PRAISE FOR
Spark THE HEART

"Nicole leads you on an engaging and informative journey exploring empathy—how and why to build your empathy muscle. Whether you feel like you're a beginner or a rock star at empathy there's something here for you."

—ALAN FINE
Founder, President of InsideOut Development

"With a solid awareness of self, Dr. Nicole Price effortlessly weaves meaningful, intimate details of her life while effectively deconstructing what it is to be empathetic—reconfiguring it in a way that defies the belief that empathy is an expendable characteristic of leadership."

—BETY LE SHACKELFORD
National Champion Synchronized Swimmer and Senior Political Strategist

"Dr. Nicole Price is an empathy revolutionary. This book is amazing! I read the foreword and could hardly wait to read the rest. Yes, we need an empathy revolution! I love the nomenclature."

—MICHELLE WIMES
Chief Equity and Inclusion Officer, Children's Mercy Hospital

"Our world is in desperate need of an 'empathy revolution.' It is the lack of empathy that demoralizes a workplace, destroys relationships, and polarizes a nation. Empathy is an essential quality for any effective leader. I can think of no one better to champion that revolution than Dr. Nicole Price. This book will help you be a better leader."

—ADAM HAMILTON,
Senior Pastor, The United Methodist Church of the Resurrection

"*Spark the Heart* is a revelation because of the brutal honesty from which it is written. Dr. Price delivers a personal account of her journey and on how to embrace empathy, what is and what it isn't, and how to unleash its potential. I found it refreshing and highly actionable. Even for someone like me, who perhaps thinks of myself as very empathetic, it was eye opening! It allows us to see the world with a deeper understanding of our own vulnerabilities and how practicing being more empathetic can become a greater strength for a better world."

—JULIÁN ZUGAZAGOITIA
Menefee D. and Mary Louise Blackwell Director and CEO, The Nelson-Atkins Museum of Art

"Dr. Price hits the ball out of the park yet again with her transparent and interactive style. She shows why empathy is good for business, both with clients and employees. Throughout, she leads the reader through activities to help in developing the qualities within themselves. This book is a must-have for all levels of management and should be required reading for all business classes!"

—SUSAN BRO
Activist, Speaker, and Writer

"Dr. Price's honesty and vulnerability is astounding and shows us that empathy comes in different forms and understanding. No matter where you are on your journey, it is like having a friend guiding you through without judgment. A remarkable, introspective exploration of how we can understand each other better."

—HALEY L. MOSS, ESQ.
Haley Moss LLC

"Dr. Price's book reminds us of the importance of empathy and helps us to understand that it is not just something you have but something you develop through intention and skill development. Her courage inspires us to be more empathetic, and her book outlines practical approaches to build this skill set within an organization."

—DON HALL, JR.
Executive Chairman of Hallmark Cards

Spark THE HEART

DR. NICOLE PRICE

Spark

THE

HEART

ENGINEERING EMPATHY
IN YOUR ORGANIZATION

Forbes | Books

Published by Forbes Books, Charleston, South Carolina.
Member of Advantage Media.

Forbes Books is a registered trademark, and the Forbes Books colophon is a trademark of Forbes Media, LLC.

Printed in the United States of America.

10 9 8 7 6 5 4 3 2 1

ISBN: 979-8-88750-096-6 (Hardcover)
ISBN: 979-8-88750-097-3 (eBook)

LCCN: 2022919562

Cover design by Amanda Haskin.
Layout design by Analisa Smith.

This custom publication is intended to provide accurate information and the opinions of the author in regard to the subject matter covered. It is sold with the understanding that the publisher, Forbes Books, is not engaged in rendering legal, financial, or professional services of any kind. If legal advice or other expert assistance is required, the reader is advised to seek the services of a competent professional.

Since 1917, Forbes has remained steadfast in its mission to serve as the defining voice of entrepreneurial capitalism. Forbes Books, launched in 2016 through a partnership with Advantage Media, furthers that aim by helping business and thought leaders bring their stories, passion, and knowledge to the forefront in custom books. Opinions expressed by Forbes Books authors are their own. To be considered for publication, please visit **books.Forbes.com**.

To my mama, Sister Gertrude Price, I love you and miss your listening ear and empathetic heart.

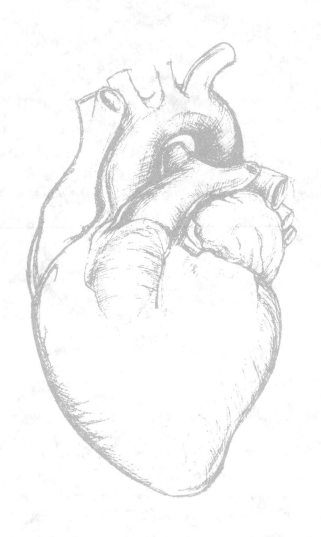

Contents

FOREWORD 1

CHAPTER 1 3
Why I Might Be the Worst Person
to Tell You about Empathy

CHAPTER 2 15
What Empathy Isn't

CHAPTER 3 31
So, What Is Empathy?

CHAPTER 4 63
Who Benefits? Yes, You!

CHAPTER 5 81
Enough Already! Setting Boundaries

CHAPTER 6 101
Let's Build Your Empathy Muscle

CHAPTER 7 121
Leading with Empathy Makes You Stronger

CONCLUSION 151
Join the Empathy Revolution

GETTING STARTED. 157

WEEK ONE: 158
Notice Empathy

WEEK TWO: 175
Practice Empathy

I GOT WORK TO DO 193

ABOUT THE AUTHOR 197

Foreword

Dr. Price's courage to seek understanding, her curiosity to learn, interest in personal development and desire to share with others have been the characteristics I have known in her since we first met early in her career after joining Hallmark. I was struck by her eagerness to learn from everyone she encountered and by her desire to enable others' success. I can't remember whether she reached out to me, or I to her, but we developed a mentoring relationship during those early years in her career. While always trying to challenge her, I always came away from our periodic meetings feeling challenged by her inquisitive spirit and eagerness to understand what could make organizations more effective, inclusive of other's differences and how to develop group norms that engender fairness and foster commitment.

As I knew her then, Nicole had a voracious appetite to learn, grow and magnify her impact. When she first spoke to me about the idea of spreading her wings by taking on a very challenging role with another corporation, my first reaction was to try to talk her out of leaving Hallmark. As I reflected on the person I had come to know, I realized that she had to follow her passion to learn and experience new work environments. Over the years, I've watched her gain many more business experiences, earn a Doctorate and become a consummate practitioner in building more effective teams.

Dr. Price shares important insights in her book, *Spark the Heart: Engineering Empathy in the Workplace.* This book reminds us of the importance of empathy and helps us to understand that it is not just something you have but is something you develop through intention and skill development. Her courage inspires us to be more empathetic and her book outlines practical approaches to build this skill set within an organization. Dr. Price shares practical and memorable examples making this book an invaluable tool for more effective teams.

Over the last several years, we have seen a growing deficit of empathy in so many areas of our lives. Dr. Price shows us how this necessary skill can make teams more successful and people personally fulfilled.

I hope you are as inspired by it as I am.

Don Hall, Jr.
Executive Chairman, Hallmark Cards Inc.

Chapter 1

Why I Might Be the Worst Person to Tell You about Empathy

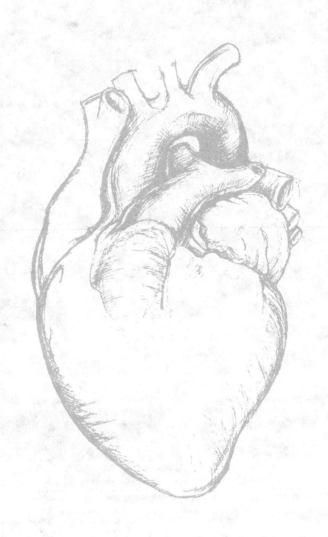

You will learn pleasantly or painfully.

—ERMA WILLIAMS

The day my mother died, I was teaching a workshop about the importance of having difficult conversations. I was on a high as I read the glowing reviews of the workshop participants when the ring of my phone changed everything. It was my sister.

Grace: "Nicole, we've been in an accident. I'm still crushed inside the car, but they are saying Mom didn't make it."

Me: "Where are you? I'm on my way."

One of my coworkers was in the area and overheard the commotion. She went with me to the nearby trauma center. There I was greeted by a chaplain who asked me, "Gertrude Price *was* your mother?"

Was—that's all I could take in. My mother was truly gone. In the weeks and months that followed, my life was like anyone else's who unexpectedly lost their parent. There were affairs to settle, arrangements to make, and a lifetime of adjustments to consider. But in a very tangible way, our situation was different. A drunk driver had killed my mother, and amid our grief, we were quickly thrust into a murder trial, one that would drag on for five years.

There isn't a person who has ever walked this earth who means more to me than my mother did. I will always and forever be grateful for her mothering. When she found out she was pregnant with me, she knew exactly what she was getting into. At thirty years old and serving thousands of people every day as a cafeteria worker, my mother was already making plenty of sacrifices—often with achy feet. I was the sixth child she had birthed since she had gotten married at sixteen. Nevertheless, she gave me access to lots of things she had never had.

She made sure that I knew she believed I was talented. Whether it was true or not, she wouldn't allow me to waste that talent. Even in areas where I was less than skilled, she was an encourager. Every morning, I would awaken her at 5:00 a.m. with my howling. She listened no matter how awful it sounded. When I left for college, she even told me she missed my "singing." Every day she cooked breakfast for me before school knowing she would have a full day of relentless emotional and physical labor.

Real breakfast.

Every day.

It wasn't until I had my own child that I realized how much work this type of consistency required. As an adult, I trusted my mother with everything. The keys to my house, the rights to my work, access to my bank accounts, and the care of my child if anything ever happened to me. I believed that I would die before she would. I think somewhere deep inside I believed that the world could easily do without me. But how could the world do without my mother? I couldn't fathom it.

Yet for everything my mother was, she was also the source of why I wanted to get as far away from empathy as possible.

My mother would feed anyone who came by. Do you understand what that means when you live in the heart of the city? Throughout the course of a day, easily fifty to sixty people could stop by! With food as the catalyst, she had many opportunities to hear people's stories. While people were in jail, she would listen to their stories of con-

6

version. When they would get out of jail, she would listen to their stories of redemption (or not). Silently, she would simply listen, rarely responding. This was my life growing up, and it continued after I had grown and moved out. When I would return to her house for a visit, I was frequently shocked and anxious after only five minutes of just sitting at the table and listening to her listen to other people's stories of betrayal, violence, poverty, heartbreak, illness, death, you name it.

It was all too much for me.

But she could do this all day, every day. Sometimes she would be on the phone talking to my grandmother, and my grandmother would describe the challenges people faced living in rural Mississippi. They would have conversations for hours about people and their problems hundreds of miles away, and my mother would just listen. Always attentive, she would then add those people to her prayer list.

I thought she needed boundaries. I wanted her to tell people they were making bad choices. I wanted her to let them know after the third (or fourth or fifth) incident that she wasn't going to listen anymore. I just could not understand how anybody could listen to all those problems, reasons, stories, and excuses and keep calmly smiling. Mostly, I would describe her reaction as centered and measured throughout. Witnessing my mother's endless capacity to care—a trait that I thought was wasted on people who were making bad choices, people who were taking advantage of my mother—I built a shield of armor around my own heart. I even built a lack of ability to listen. Unlike my mother, I began to view the world solely with objectivity. I constantly asked myself . . .

What would I want to happen if I were *not* involved?

What would I want to happen if I *didn't* know these people?

What are people on the other side of the world doing who *know nothing* of this issue right now?

I started to perceive myself as separate and apart from the community of people I was surrounded by. It is devastating to think about now. Today, I offer myself a lot of empathy and compassion. It helps me walk through that devastation and get to a different side—a more empathetic side. The boundaries I had set were in part how I was able to make it through some pretty trying times in my life. People who lack empathy, as I once did, share the belief that they can get a ton accomplished when they don't concern themselves with "people issues." It is common for them to think that lacking empathy just might provide the buoyancy to results rather than the barrier.

> People who lack empathy, as I once did, share the belief that they can get a ton accomplished when they don't concern themselves with "people issues."

But the tragedy is that sometimes we need to take a subjective view. We need to humanize the people in front of us. We need to step into situations and ask, "What would I want to happen if it were me?"

"What does *this person* need most right now?"

I spent much of my life stepping away from people, not toward them. But my mother's example, which once pushed me to step away, has now helped me to find my way back. Remembering how she would think about my great-grandmother's experiences that may have caused her to not be so loving, I understand how, with lifelong scars on her arms from the abuse, my mom managed to still demonstrate for me what it means to try to understand other people. Watching her feed hungry people and relish the simple joy of watching them eat delicious food, I had an example of what it looks like to prioritize people over policy and practice. She could've easily chosen to feed only her children. She could have chosen to support only institutions, like food banks, which have greater resources to feed people. But she did not. Every day I saw her demonstrate that it cost us nothing to listen and to give an empathetic ear to people who are in need and people who need nothing from us.

When my mother died, I was asked to give our family's victim impact statement at the pretrial hearings of the man who had killed her. I cried so hard I could barely get my words out. Even in my grief, I wondered how I would be judged for being empathetic. I knew then that people do not expect or celebrate empathy when they believe people do not deserve it. Certainly, people would not only understand the absence of empathy for the man who killed my mother, they would expect it. Yet I felt compelled to share in our statement that my mother would have considered the perpetrator's point of view. She would have thought about the fact that her assailant had not woken up that morning intending to kill her. She would have pondered what his life was like in a foster care system that lacked empathy and compassion. Mom would have thought about the reality that he did not get the support necessary to tend to his own mental challenges. She even would have tried to imagine, although she never drank or did drugs, what it was like for him to try to satiate his grief using alcohol and drugs.

For these reasons, I knew that my mother would lead with empathy, not with indifference or anger. I delivered the statement, and Jonathan Ross was convicted of second-degree murder and sentenced to fifteen years in prison. It was a travesty for his mother. It was a travesty for his recently born child, who will be a teenager by the time he gets out. And I believe my mom would have thought it was a travesty too. My mother spent her life demonstrating empathy, trying to understand others, and recognizing the humanity in everyone. That day her demonstration manifested in my words and my tears. It was a pivotal moment in my understanding about empathy. The consequences of his choices did not go unpunished, but they were not punished to the greatest extent of the law, which would have been a twenty-eight-year sentence without the possibility of parole.

My most ardent critic that day? A family member who couldn't legally drive himself anywhere because he'd gotten one too many DUIs.

As I write this, I can hardly believe I have chosen to author a book that celebrates, encourages, and values empathy, because I spent the better part of forty years trying to lead with logic and reason and pushing empathy and compassion to the side. My mother's death was the beginning of me trying to right the ship.

Before she died, I thought people used her. I believed that sometimes she was codependent. There was no way you could convince me that she was not being naive at times. What I know now is that she was none of those things. Instead, she was an empathetic revolutionary. Shockingly, it became obvious to me that her life was better because of it, not worse. She recognized that our own hurt and pain diminish when we consider *what happened to* someone rather than *what is wrong* with them.

This book is a call for all of us to lean in to the demonstration of Sister Gertrude Price and show up every day with an empathetic ear and the hands to do something compassionate for someone besides ourselves.

WHY THIS BOOK?

When I considered taking on this project, I knew I wanted to focus on the work I am privileged to do every day: helping leaders be better at their jobs. The challenge is, How do I get leaders who don't believe that empathy belongs in their toolbox of leadership characteristics to read a book about empathy? I share my story and the data from my professional experiences. A story of a logical, reasonable, results-focused leader who, until a few years ago, didn't practice empathy or believe there was a need to focus on it—certainly not in the business world.

I understand why the well-meaning, logical, reasonable, results-focused leaders find it hard to comprehend why people simply cannot do their jobs. After all, they've committed themselves to these roles, so why would they need coaxing, cajoling, or hand-holding? It used to frustrate the heck out of me, too, until I recognized that commitment works both ways: employee to employer and employer to employee. If the employer is not committed to providing the employee the support, tools, and resources required to get their job done, they can't expect an employee to keep their commitment to get their job done. Conversely, for the employer to commit to providing the employee what's needed to get the job done, they must understand what those needs are. Therefore, leading with empathy matters. Empathy is critical to this mutual understanding. Contrary to what many believe, leading with empathy is not about hand-holding or making excuses. It is the opposite. Empathy is the foundation that allows us to move forward.

Leading with empathy is about understanding others and then strategically leveraging that understanding to make progress.

Yes, I used *empathy*, *strategic*, and *leverage* in the same sentence—I bet you didn't expect that. The job to be done may be getting your team to arrive on time and ready to start meetings. If your team member is scheduled at a mandated meeting across town that ends fifteen minutes before yours begins and it takes twenty minutes to get across town, they are rarely going to be on time. If you don't understand why they always arrive late (and stressed), you're not going to solve the problem. In fact, a lack of understanding will make the problem worse.

If the production level on your assembly line has dropped, how will you know that it's because the new box you introduced last week takes twenty seconds longer than the old box to assemble if you don't talk to and understand how the people on the line do their job? Empathizing with the workers in this scenario and asking for their thoughts can lead to improved production. Without that understanding, you'll end up with a supervisor uselessly yelling at the line workers to work faster, and that's not going to end well for anyone.

I use these two simple examples because I want you to think about practicing empathy in simple ways. It is a good starting point to empathetic leadership. But before we can lead with empathy, we must appreciate the value of empathy and learn to practice it in our daily lives, and we need everyone to get on board with this.

In today's world there is a significant shortage of empathy at a time when we need a surplus of it.

At the time of this writing, a greater number of young people are committing suicide. Results from the 2019 Youth Behavioral Risk Factor Surveillance System show that 3.2 million high school students seriously considered attempting suicide and 1.5 million did attempt suicide. The financial cost of suicide attempts in the United States in 2019 was estimated to be $70 billion (about $220 per person in the US),[1] but I cannot easily find the emotional cost to families. This caused me to question whether we care to understand that cost.

One in three United States citizens will be diagnosed with some form of cancer. In the last year, I have had five friends contract the disease. Two lost their battles, and one has a bladder made from her intestines that she has to "train" to behave as a bladder. One of her primary worries? How does she tell her boss that she's not ready to return to work just yet because her fake bladder is trying to kill her?

There are more mass shootings than there are days in the year. Meanwhile, our religious beliefs, our values, our general dispositions are tearing us apart. This doesn't have to be. We are together. We are not separated. Jonathan Kozol said that we should pick battles big enough to matter, small enough to win. Yet we decide to make the most trivial things matter and tend to not care who loses as long as it's not us. Sometimes we will even choose to lose if we feel justified in our beliefs. We argue to be right when we really want to be happy. It does not

> **We argue to be right when we really want to be happy.**

have to be this way. I believe that we can be more effective, and sometimes that means we find out that we were wrong.

We can make progress together with a foundation of empathy.

We can make great decisions, parent well, lead effectively, and do most things in the world that involve people and do them well if empathy is at the center of the discussion. I learned this the hard way, but I don't think the hard way has to be *the* way. Empathy can be taught, and if you stick with me, you will be able to stretch and

---

1   Centers for Disease Control and Prevention, "Youth Risk Behavior Surveillance—United States, 2019, cdc.gov, PUB August 21, 2020, https://www.cdc.gov/healthyyouth/data/yrbs/pdf/2019/su6901-H.pdf.

grow empathetically and help to stretch and grow others in the same way. You will spark an empathy revolution.

So how about we spark this empathy revolution together?

Chapter 2

What Empathy Isn't

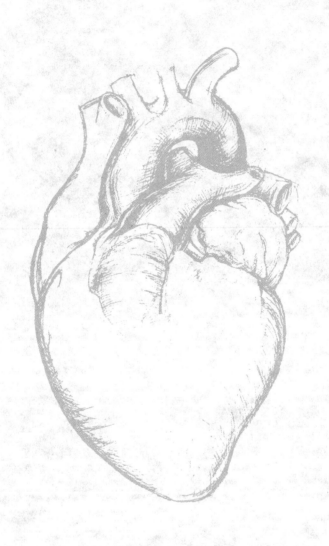

When someone is in denial about what happened,
they cannot perceive what is true.

—ERIN MERRYN

One day I was standing in the manufacturing plant with our engineering manager. The printing presses were humming. Running at one thousand feet (about the height of the Empire State Building) per minute, the "hum" was more like the sound of a freight train. There were nine machines the size of city buses lined up behind us. We were having our regular stand-up meeting, and I wasn't expecting any exciting news. That's when our manager said, "Now that Brian is gone, we're moving projects around." He kept talking, but my brain was focused on trying to catch up.

Wait, what?

Brian was my person. When had he quit, and why hadn't he told me? We had been virtually connected at the hip. The two of us strategized about how to get promoted. We laughed together as the senior engineers bragged about using slide rules for calculations instead of scientific calculators. We shared a love for fine-tipped pens and graph paper. We regularly went to lunch together when he wasn't having lunch with the safety manager, Mindy.

Immediately I understood why Gallup asked the engagement question I previously thought was ridiculous: "Do you have a best friend at work?" I panicked at the idea of not having anyone to talk to privately about the foolishness that happened in our department meetings. I needed to know what happened. When my boss finished up, I walked off the production floor and over to the central office to visit Mindy.

As I entered the office area, I was still thinking loudly, because I'd just come from the noisy machine area where my manager was practically yelling at us to be heard. Central office was eerily quiet. I approached Mindy, who sat in the middle of the administrative department. My loud thinking became my loud voice, and I nearly shouted, "Mindy, what happened to Brian?" She just stared at me.

I continued, "You're with him all the time. Why did he leave?" Whatever she said, I don't recall it. Undaunted—and when I say undaunted, I mean ignorant beyond oblivion—I continued my search for answers and called Brian, who invited me to come over to visit him and his wife.

On that visit, I learned that the person I called my "best friend at work" was having an affair with, you guessed it, Mindy. Their affair had turned ugly, an investigation ensued, and Brian had been asked to leave the company—oh, and it turns out, I was one of the very few in the office who did not know all this had transpired.

Did I empathize with Brian? Yes, I did. He was my friend, and most of us naturally want to empathize with our friends. But empathy for Brian is not what I want to convince you of. That was quite easy for me.

I want you to try to empathize with Mindy.

When I reflect on this story, I realize that I noticed something in Mindy's face. It was embarrassment. I ignored it. At the time, I wanted an answer—nothing more, nothing less. I was clueless about what she or anyone else felt about my search for those answers.

Mindy was embarrassed, and I had been embarrassed before. It is a common belief that unless you have personally experienced something, you cannot empathize with other people in those scenarios. However, it would be an excuse for me to say that without having had a work affair, there's no way I could truly empathize with Mindy. False! I know what embarrassment feels and looks like. If I had simply taken a moment to pay attention, I would have understood and used a different approach.

In all, the truth is that I had not intended to embarrass Mindy. My friendship was with Brian, and we remained friends for years. I also remained as cordial as I had always been with Mindy. All these things were true. However, the rational thinking that presumes that everything is within limits if you believe it to be true can be damaging if you aren't also aware of the impact

Today, I think about the impact of my decisions as well as the intent.

your "truth" has on other people. Today, I think about the impact of my decisions as well as the intent.

I haven't even told you the rest of the Brian and Mindy story yet, but what I will share with you now is that even when I heard all the facts, I dug into my objective reasoning. I avoided trying to understand how the people involved might have been feeling. Because of how I operated at that time, I was satisfied knowing where Brian was and why he was no longer working at the same company as me. That was all the information I required to be on my way. No aha moment, no light bulb going off, not even a thread of awareness that I should step back and wonder how I did not know that my work best friend was struggling with something until after he had left. I also hadn't given any thought to how I might have made Mindy feel now that I knew the circumstances.

When I think back, I am amazed at how oblivious I was to what was going on in the lives of the people around me. In fact, I'm embarrassed to say, I wasn't just oblivious. I took it a step further and invited other leaders to join me in my efforts. As a global consultant I created the space for other leaders to ignore their impact on their teammates. It wasn't overt. I hid it under the guise of not arguing with "reality."

I spent years of my life as a keynote speaker espousing reality-based leadership "rules of the workplace." I was telling leaders to ditch the drama and take no excuses, and that yes, in fact, there is such a thing as a stupid question. One of our team's famous lines on the speaking circuit was, "When should you fire a person? The moment you think of it." My audience was full of human resources personnel. They would laugh and laud me afterward for my great presentations and for saying what needed to be said. Yes, you read that right: people working in human resources ate up my take-no-prisoners-tell-the-truth-regardless leadership methods.

Here are a couple of other "wisdoms" I, devoid of empathy, would damagingly spout off:

- **Stop surveying the victims.** Yes, you might have to survey everybody, but get the real opinions of the top-performing 20 percent of your employees. Ask this group, "What should the company do? What do you think about this?" and forget the other 80 percent.

- **Engage or leave.** The biggest complaint of top performers is that there is no differentiation between them and the disengaged. The message for the disengaged crowd? Engage or leave. Tell them, "You think there's a third option, but there's not."

These two perspectives are the opposite of empathetic leadership. Yet for thousands of people, I was one of the ones encouraging them. There is no telling how much damage was done. So, why am I being transparent about this? I think it is important that you know I was terrible at empathy. I am a convert, not a natural.

I know it's hard to practice empathy.

I have spent years of my life, not moments, in the absence of empathy—both the absence of giving empathy and the absence of receiving empathy. The latter is wildly important because I believe that the least empathetic people are the ones who don't practice empathy toward themselves either. Furthermore, now I have spent years developing my empathy muscle, which has helped me to be more effective. It has also improved the working lives of everyone who has worked with me. And because at heart I am a scientist, I take the liberty to say that if a chemical engineer with few natural empathetic tendencies can learn to be empathetic, anyone can. If you already practice empathy—great, let's talk about how you can make your empathy muscle stronger and help others develop theirs. If you don't practice empathy and you don't believe in the potential benefits of empathy, stick around to find out how this logical, rational scientist became an empathy crusader. Just know that I have an objective—to persuade you to join me.

Where to begin? First let's talk about what empathy isn't and dispel some of the myths that surround it.

You may believe that either you have empathy or you don't, or that empathy is something only weak leaders employ. Perhaps you think that most people exploit empathetic people. You might

> **Any time anyone has ever tried to get someone to understand them, they were seeking empathy.**

even believe that you don't have a need for empathy, have never needed empathy, but I guarantee you have. Any time anyone has ever tried to get someone to understand them, they were seeking empathy. Think about these moments in your own life. Did the person offer you the understanding you were seeking? If they did, how did you benefit from their gift of empathy?

EMPATHY MYTHS DEBUNKED

---

1. ## Empathy is a trait that you're born with or not.

    While some people are naturally more empathetic, empathy is a skill that is learned over a lifetime of experience, learning, and practice.

2. ## Empathy is just one thing.

    Empathy involves the many ways we respond to each other. The distinct types of empathy that we engage in activate various parts of our brain—yes, there is science to empathy, which leads us to our next myth.

3. ## Empathy is just fluff.

    Empathy has been well documented and proved to be an essential component for mental health, innovation, engagement, retention, inclusivity, and work-life fulfillment.

4. ## Empathy requires you to adopt the other person's beliefs and values.

    Empathy is not believing another's beliefs or living another's values. Empathy is understanding why another person believes what they believe and values what they value, even if it's different from your own.

5. Empathy is feeling sorry for another person.

Empathy is understanding and being sensitive to another person's thoughts, feelings, and experiences; it is not commiserating with another person, which is based on your own thoughts, feelings, and experiences. While there are times to feel sorry for people, that is not the definition of empathy.

6. Empathy makes you weak.

Empathy takes the courage to acknowledge and sit with your own difficult feelings so that you can better understand and connect with those around you. Connecting to others strengthens relationships and has been shown to reduce depression and anxiety.[2]

7. You can't always practice empathy.

Yes, you can. Empathy does not require action. It is the simple act of trying to understand and get into the shoes of another person. Your ability to respond better is improved as your level of understanding expands.

8. Empathy is give, give, give.

This debunking involves three components:

- While empathy can feel overwhelming at times, healthy empathy requires boundaries. You might burn out if you try

---

2 Virginia C. Salo, "Depressive symptoms in parents are associated with reduced empathy toward their young children," ncbi.nlm.nih.gov, Pub March 23, 2020, https://www.ncbi.nlm.nih.gov/pmc/articles/PMC7089529/.
Sun Mi Choi, Jinwoo Lee, Young Sik Park, Chang-Hoon Lee, Sang-Min Lee, Jae-Joon Yim, "Effect of Verbal Empathy and Touch on Anxiety Relief in Patients Undergoing Flexible Bronchoscopy: Can Empathy Reduce Patients' Anxiety?," Karger.com, May 21, 2016, https://www.karger.com/Article/Fulltext/450960.

to understand the feelings and circumstances of everyone around you twenty-four hours a day.

- Acting with empathy provides benefits to the empathizer too. For starters, it helps you understand and regulate your own emotions and promotes better connections with others.

- You aren't always the empathizer. You have been on the receiving end of empathy from those you choose to spend time with.

9. Empathy doesn't belong at work.

Inattention and lack of empathy can cause people to misinterpret what other people are trying to say, which can lead to miscommunication, conflict, and damaged relationships—how are any of those helpful in a work environment?

Empathy most definitely belongs in the workplace.

10. Empathy means that you don't have high expectations and stretch goals.

If you are doing incredible work in the world, you will have lofty expectations and clear goals. This is not separate and apart from empathy. In fact, empathy can fuel these expectations and aspirations.

"The top 10 companies in the Global Empathy Index 2015 increased in value more than twice as much as the bottom 10 and generated 50 percent more earnings (defined by market capitalization). In our work with clients, we have found a correlation as high as 80 percent between departments with higher empathy and those with high performers."[3]

And "eighty-seven percent of CEOs believe a company's financial performance is tied to empathy in the workplace, as do 79 percent of HR professionals."[4]

Identifying the falsity of these myths did not happen for me overnight. It was a process. A process that I am grateful to Dr. Ian A. Roberts, author of *Radical Empathy in Leadership*, for igniting.

3   Belinda Parmar, "The Most Empathetic Companies, 2016," hbr.org, December 1, 2016, https://hbr.org/2016/12/the-most-and-least-empathetic-companies-2016.

4   Businessolver, "Businessolver Quantifies Empathy In The Workplace: 87 Percent Of CEOs Agree That A Company's Financial Performance Is Tied To Empathy," prnewswire.com, April 12, 2018, https://www.prnewswire.com/news-releases/ businessolver-quantifies-empathy-in-the-workplace-87-percent-of-ceos-agree-that- a-companys-financial-performance-is-tied-to-empathy-300628497.html

DUDE, YOU SHOULD JUST FIRE EVERYONE

"Nicole, we are doing exactly what you told us to do, and the employees are staging a coup. They are threatening a union walkout." That's the call I received from one of my reality-based leadership clients.

"I'm on my way," I assured them and booked the next available flight. While sitting in the airport, I overheard the conversation of a gentleman sitting nearby. He looked incredibly fit in his vibrant three-piece suit. He had an accent I could not place and often struggled to understand, but it was clear to me that *he* was trying to convince people to do what *they* said they were going to do. He was reminding them of *their* commitments, trying to hold them accountable to *their* responsibilities, not his, and they didn't seem to be moving.

When he hung up, I offered my unsolicited advice: "Dude, you should just fire everybody. None of those people seem like they're committed to the work."

He laughed and asked me when I thought a leader should fire someone.

You already know my answer. I told him, "The moment you think of it."

We laughed.

And that is how I was introduced to Dr. Ian A. Roberts. That day he went on to explain the challenging environment in which he worked, and how it could be extremely difficult, even dangerous, for the people involved to rigidly stick to their commitments. The more he told me, the more I thought *he* should leave and find a place to work where people cared about the mission of the organization.

We exchanged contact information, but I was thinking, "Just get a whole new team and start over. I don't know why anybody would be involved with it." Then off I went to try to ward off my client's impending coup.

I arrived at the facility for my gemba walk. *Gemba* means to go and see the real place. It is a continuous-improvement practice of leaders walking the floors of where the actual work is taking place to observe employees and processes. Within five minutes of observation, I realized, Holy crap, management doesn't empathize with the line workers. They think they are better than them, they have zero awareness of their employees' lived experiences, they have no experience doing or even understanding their employees' jobs, and yet they are dumbfounded as to why these people aren't the happiest workers in the world. It was clear to me why rage was bubbling up. Employees were now being forced to take full responsibility for every aspect of their jobs, but the leaders weren't holding up their end of the bargain.

I was mortified.

Even simple, logical steps were not taken. For example, there was no available water for the employees working in the sweltering warehouse! I pulled the plant manager and operations manager into the conference room, and I drew Patrick Lencioni's pyramid on the whiteboard. I showed them that first, it is their responsibility to build trust with their employees, then encouraged them to engage in healthy conflict. Then, I went on to explain, once people trust that they can express themselves and feel like they've been understood, they will commit to what is required of them. This all leads to accountability, which leads to results. Regretfully, I was at fault. I was the one who had taught them an entire workshop about how to hard wire accountability on teams. However, you can't "hard wire accountability" with people who can't even trust you to make sure they don't die from heat exhaustion!

I pointed to the bottom half of the pyramid drawing and said, "You all have skipped steps one, two, *and* three, then jumped to four. You can't do that. You must build the foundation before you can expect accountability." They got it right away, thankfully, but there was a lot of work to be done, and I called on my new friend, Dr. Roberts, to help me help them build the foundation.

This encounter was the beginning of me understanding the ugliness that can occur in the absence of empathy. It was also the spark in a series of life-altering events that placed me on my professional empathy journey. However, building empathy does not require a major, life-altering event; you can, through practice, build the skill at any point in your life. In building my empathy skills, I have come to personally experience what psychologists have known scientifically for centuries: empathy is a strength, not a weakness. It can be built and developed, and it's critically

> Empathy is a strength, not a weakness.

important for us to strengthen our empathy muscle if we are to create the world that many of us aspire to live in and leave behind.

Before we begin to break down how to build empathy, let's talk in more detail about what empathy is and the lessons I learned from Dr. Roberts and hundreds of clients.

Chapter 3

So, What Is Empathy?

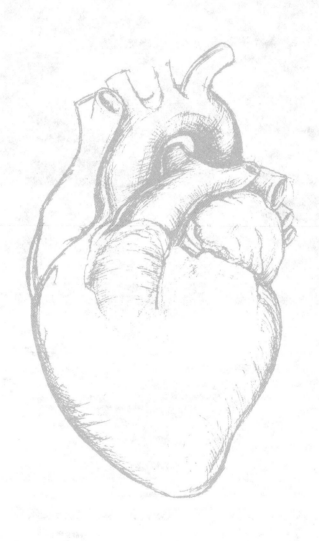

*I think we all have empathy. We may not
have enough courage to display it.*

— MAYA ANGELOU

Remember Brian and Mindy? My involvement in that story didn't end when Brian left. Mindy and I continued to work for the same company over the next five years. Our jobs didn't overlap much, but I did have occasion to email and/or converse with her about work matters now and again. That was until I got a special project opportunity designed to encourage people to join our organization; in this case, it was engineers and technical professionals. That meant I needed backup for my job at the plant while I was gone, and Mindy volunteered to help.

I was traveling all the time and having a blast. Mindy would often send emails asking questions and sending updates. I did notice that for every email she sent, she also copied my boss, Ed. Workload sharing had been in full swing for a couple of months, and one day, I received this snippy email from Mindy, and I thought, "What the hell is her problem?" At the first opportunity, I invited her to join me in a conference room. By this point my blood was boiling, and by the look on Mindy's face when she entered the conference room, I could see hers was too.

Me: "What's your problem? The tone of your emails is nasty, and why are you copying Ed on everything?"

She turned to me and said, "You embarrassed me! You knew the situation between Brian and me, and you came up to the front office, practically yelling, 'Where is Brian?' I know you did it on purpose in front of everyone."

The last five years of interactions with her went flashing through my mind. I wondered how I'd missed the signs of her rage.

She had been sitting with this anger and hurt for five years. In every interaction we had during that time, she was thinking about how she hated my guts and how awful I was. Meanwhile, once I had had my answers about Brian, the entire incident was out of my mind—completely. I hadn't thought of it once while Mindy was stewing. It took me a second, but I quickly caught on.

Once I did catch up, empathizing with her was a bit easier this time, because I had since gone through a divorce that was partially because of my own husband's cheating.

One might think that I would be even more terse with Mindy, considering that in this scenario, I was the equivalent of Brian's wife. Instead, in that moment I put myself in Mindy's shoes. I leaned in to what it felt like to be embarrassed. I remembered the part of my story when I returned home from a trip to find my husband and half of our belongings gone. The man had even taken the ice cream scoop!

I felt humiliated.

Because of my own personal experience, I could now empathize with Mindy's embarrassment and humiliation regardless of whether I agreed with her decisions. It was easy for me to let her know that I honestly hadn't known what had happened before I so bluntly demanded she tell me where Brian was.

When I tell this story, people who've been betrayed get angry with me. To them it feels like I am validating Mindy's experience. Questioning my morality, they ask me, "What about Brian's wife?" First of all, love her!

I have no issues with Brian's wife and was quite supportive of her. Second, this ain't my relationship. Relationships are complicated, at times messy, and I have my own relationships to manage. Third, it is Brian's work to be loyal to his wife. My work is to acknowledge the inherent dignity in every person I interact with. I have the right to judge the morality of anyone's actions at any time. Many times, I do, but I am often reminded that other people have the right to judge the morality of my actions too. I don't typically enjoy it when the judgment is directed toward me.

Here's the empathy challenge: no matter what a person has done, taking an empathetic view has the propensity to spark us to higher-level thinking and better behavior. I cannot control Mindy, Brian, or anyone else. I *can* control myself and my actions. My choices can make matters better or worse. Remember that I recognized embarrassment in Mindy's face and *chose* to carry on when I could have responded differently. I did not need to agree with her to humanize instead of demonize her. Did I need the *same* experience as Mindy to empathize with her? I did not. Besides, this book isn't about you

> No matter what a person has done, taking an empathetic view has the propensity to spark us to higher-level thinking and better behavior.

choosing sides in a marital triangle. This book is about you being empathetic to the people you work with. Think about someone at your job with whom you find it impossible to work. Did they sleep with your partner? Likely not! It's more probable that you're mad because they do petty things that annoy you. Trivial things that aren't worth being annoyed about. What could happen if we practiced empathy with the trivial things?

SO, WHAT IS EMPATHY?

Dr. Edward Titchener coined the English word *empathy* from the Greek root word for empathy, which is *empatheia*. *Empatheia* means passion and was adapted to German to mean feeling. In its simplest form, empathy is having an awareness and general sense of the emotions of other people. It is the ability to understand what others are feeling and imagine what they may be experiencing. Armed with this insight, empathetic people can respond appropriately.

Many people equate empathy with caring. When the topic of empathy comes up, it's common for people to think, "Now you expect me to care about everyone—what they're doing, how they're feeling. I don't have time for that." While caring is often a natural consequence of practicing empathy, the truth is caring is not required. Understanding is. When you start with understanding, you might begin to care about the person's plight.

I mentioned that I am a scientist. As such, if I write about empathy in the simplest form without acknowledging the complexities, the people who have studied empathy all their lives might want to skewer me. Therefore, it is important to know that there are several types of empathy, which include affective, cognitive, compassionate, somatic, and radical. All are useful for leaders. Here's the breakdown.

AFFECTIVE EMPATHY

Affective empathy is the ability to emotionally respond appropriately to people and situations. Affective empathy is sharing an emotional experience, a sense of feeling together. If someone is indifferent when they observe other people experiencing hardships, they may lack affective empathy.

Affective Empathy versus Indifference: It's Your Choice

You walk into the nursing home to visit your grandmother and find her in her room with an aide. The aide has just finished brushing your grandmother's hair and is asking her which lipstick she would like her to apply. Your grandmother has always taken pride in her appearance, and the aide knows this, and so she always takes time to help your grandmother put on "her face" and pick out her clothes each morning. Your grandmother's smile could not be any brighter.

Think about the emotions you feel in this moment. Can you feel what your grandmother feels? What about the aide? What might they feel? Can you name the emotions? Do you share some of the same emotions?

I think most of us would agree that this scenario is how our mothers, fathers, grandparents, and, one day, each of us would want to be treated when we live under the care of others. And yet … the care our elders receive in assisted living and nursing facilities often lacks this type of affective empathy. Instead, we find indifference.

What if, instead, this was the scenario?

You walk into the nursing home to visit your grandmother, and you arrive at her room just as an aide is wheeling her out into the hall. Your grandmother, who has always taken such pride in her appearance, is disheveled. Her clothes are wrinkled and stained; her hair is uncombed; and her glasses, which sit crooked on her face, are covered in smudges. You kindly ask the aide to please help take care of your grandmother's hair, glasses, etc., to which the aide responds, "Oh, I don't have time for that this morning," and pushes your grandmother past you on their way to the dining room.

How do your emotions change when you consider this scenario? What might your grandmother feel in this situation? The aide? Was it easier or harder for you to name the emotions using this scenario? Before you named the emotions, did you start to use the cognitive parts of your brain to think instead of feel? Thinking is good. However, thinking *and* feeling is better. It is what keeps us from becoming indifferent to the issues of the day.

As a society, we have built up a tremendous amount of indifference for our elders. A separation so wide that we don't bother to notice the value of our senior population or recognize them as individuals filled with lifetimes of joy, grief, love, and accomplishments.

Our COVID response for seniors displayed our lack of empathy on steroids. Here are just a few media statements that show just how indifferent we have become:

Australia:

"We've grown too big for our own good, now nature replies by thinning us out a bit. At the end of all this, we will be stronger as a group, with elderly and sick no longer being a burden" (chat room posting, *Sydney Morning Herald*, April 22, 2020).

"Provide government support to help the 70s+ stay at home but don't wreck the economy along with millions of jobs and lives" (letter to *The Age*, March 25, 2020).

United Kingdom:

"Pensioners? Meh, they've had a good run"; "Old people are an increasing burden, but must our young ones be the ones to shoulder it?" (postings to *The Guardian*, April 26 and May 8, 2020).

United States:

"When did all this become about not losing a single life to the virus? Everyone will die someday; People who are older are going to be susceptible to Covid-19. Hope it's worth putting a bullet in the economy to try to head off" (postings to the *New York Times*, May 8, 2020).[5]

We choose to perceive our elders as drastically different from us, but here's the thing: our elders are our future selves. Yes, we can spend the next twenty, thirty, forty years of our life in ignorance, pretending that we will never be them—but if we live long enough, we will. Which scenario do you hope for when you need the care of others?

If we can imagine every elder person is our mother, father, grandparent, future self, the gap closes, and affective empathy takes hold.

---

5   Bronwen Lichtenstein, "From 'Coffin Dodger' to 'Boomer Remover': Outbreaks of Ageism in Three Countries with Divergent Approaches to Coronavirus Control," National Library of Medicine, July 28, 2020, https://www.ncbi.nlm.nih.gov/pmc/articles/PMC7454844/

COGNITIVE EMPATHY

Cognitive empathy is the ability to understand what a person is thinking and feeling without necessarily resonating with that thinking or feeling state. Cognitive empathy is necessary to overcome our inherent biases. Because of the way our brains are wired, people who look or act like us or have had similar life experiences are the ones we naturally share a sense of "togetherness" with (affective empathy), and those who don't look or act like us or have similar life experiences we may unconsciously view as a threat.

"People are evolutionarily wired to recognize and respond to differences, and socially or culturally based perceptions can trigger subconscious fears that threaten emotional [stability]."[6]

Cognitive empathy helps us neutralize our "wired" biases so that we don't shut out those we may not naturally relate to. Cognitive empathy is critical for healthcare workers and their ability to provide compassionate care to all.

Using Your Brain to Provide Compassionate Care

A pediatric oncology clinician who shows tremendous empathy for her young patients might not be able to provide that same level of affective empathy if she were working in the mental health field with

---

6   Helen Reiss, MD, "The Science of Empathy," ncbi.nlm.nih.gov, June 4, 2017, https://www.ncbi.nlm.nih.gov/pmc/articles/PMC5513638/.

adults who were addicted to drugs. This same clinician may not be able to emotionally connect with the challenges of addictions due to her own unconscious biases—a "'they' shouldn't have gotten themselves addicted in the first place" kind of thought process. To provide compassionate care to the individuals overcoming addictions, she will need to draw on her cognitive empathy to bridge the emotional gap. If she can't emotionally connect, she should think about what she would want to happen if it were her in the situation.

The same is true for a nurse who decides that the patient who is six feet tall and 250 pounds and is complaining about his pain is just acting like a baby and doesn't really need more medication. Her bias that big, strong men should be tougher than their pain will make it difficult to supply the same level of compassionate care that she offers her petite, eighty-six-year-old female patients if cognitive empathy is not employed.

COMPASSIONATE EMPATHY

Compassionate empathy is both the understanding of another's pain and the desire to somehow mitigate that pain through acts of kindness, caring, and support. This includes being motivated to engage in social behavior that helps other people or society as a whole. Avoiding helping people who are upset, hurt, or at a disadvantage shows a lack of compassion.

Education Builds Understanding

Valerie Nicholson-Watson, former president and CEO of Harvesters—The Community Food Network, knows all about the power of compassion and the importance of its origin of understanding:

> *I was having a discussion with a woman who controlled charitable dollars, and I shared with her that seniors are the fastest-growing segment of the population to be food insecure. Her comment was, "It's a shame that they didn't plan better."*
>
> *I was dumbfounded and thought, "Oh my goodness, if this person has been so involved from a philanthropic perspective with this organization and they still don't understand, still can't empathize with those we serve, we have some work to do." We put a lot of effort into educating the people who volunteer for us so that they understand why food insecurity exists and they understand who is food insecure. This interaction made me realize that there is a category of people who we need to share information with a little differently so that they, too, come from a place of understanding.*
>
> *If you have always been financially stable enough that you haven't had to worry about paying your bills and you had enough to also save for the future, then without education and awareness, you may not understand that future financial planning is not that simple for all of us. There are people who struggle to make ends meet throughout their adult life, leaving no money available to save for the future. I think the pandemic forced us all into awareness of this reality. When we talked about our essential workers outside the healthcare arena, people began to recognize the other essential roles people play in our community—we want*

our grocery stores open and the cashiers to be there, we want our farm and manufacturing workers to make sure the product we want is available, we want waitstaff to still wait on us, and we want it even if it means they are all put at a higher risk. The pandemic put a spotlight on how essential and hardworking these people are and how little money they make. These are the people who must go to the food pantry to stretch their dollars. The pandemic made us a little more generous in our empathy because it gave us a truer picture of who is hungry and why and the choices that they sometimes must make, because the bottom line is, the workers who keep our communities running don't have enough resources to meet their daily needs.

The better people understand who and why, the more empowered they are to act, which includes sharing their understanding with others, which leads to more empathy plus action.

If "doing good" action isn't connected to empathy, misinformation can develop and spread, impeding the opportunities for nonprofits to reach people who need their services.

What is charity if you are motivated to act based on your belief that the person is only in need because of their "bad planning"? How generous and helpful can you be if you have the separating belief that you would never be in that predicament? Empathy and compassion are quite different. They are even controlled by different areas of the brain. With empathy, we join the suffering of others who suffer but stop short of actually helping. With compassion, we take a step away from the emotion of empathy and ask ourselves, "How can we help?" Therefore, I am a fan of compassionate empathy, especially toward the needy or suffering.

SOMATIC EMPATHY

Somatic empathy is the ability to physically feel changes in your body when you observe the emotions of others.

When the Unthinkable Happens

On May 24, 2022, two teachers and nineteen boys and girls aged nine and ten were gunned down at Robb Elementary School in Uvalde, Texas. Nearly four hundred officers rushed to the school but waited more than an hour to confront the eighteen-year-old shooter in a fourth-grade classroom.

One dad reported, "There were five or six of (us) fathers, hearing the gunshots, and (police officers) were telling us to move back," he told the paper. "We didn't care about us. We wanted to storm the building. We were saying, 'Let's go' because that is how worried we were, and we wanted to get our babies out." Hours later, he learned his daughter had been shot and killed.[7]

When you watched the events unfold or read about the aftermath in the paper, did your breathing change? Did you feel panic rise in your chest? Did you feel like your skin was crawling?

When you heard and saw with the rest of the world that police did nothing for a solid hour while the children were being gunned

---

7   Holly Yan, Harmeet Kaur, Melissa Alonso, Amir Vera, Sharif Paget, "What we know about the victims at Robb Elementary School," cnn.com, July 22, 2022, https://www.cnn.com/2022/05/25/us/victims-uvalde-texas-school-shooting/index.html.

down, did nausea settle in your stomach, did it reach the back of your throat? Did your face grow hot with outrage?

You were, on some level, physically feeling the horror the parents were experiencing.

Body Scan

We hold trauma, even secondary trauma, in our bodies. Body scanning can help if you feel it so deeply that you cannot function.

Let's do a body scan.

Body scanning involves paying attention to parts of the body and bodily sensations in a gradual sequence from feet to head. By mentally scanning yourself, you bring awareness to every single part of your body, noticing any aches, pains, tension, or general discomfort.

Pay attention to your physical reactions to the emotions and circumstances of others. Be aware of the sensations of your breath. Feel your breath going in and out of your nostrils and passing through the back of your throat. Feel the chest or belly rising and falling.

When you're ready, move your awareness down the left leg, past the knee and ankle and right down into the big toe of your left foot. Notice the sensations in your big toe with a sense of curiosity. Is it warm or cold?

Now expand your awareness to your little toe, then all the toes in between. What do they feel like? If you can't feel any sensation, that's okay. As you breathe in, imagine the breath going down your body and into your toes. As you breathe out, imagine the breath going back up your body and out of your nose. Use this strategy of breathing into and out of each part to which you're paying attention.

RADICAL EMPATHY

Radical empathy is the relentless commitment to fundamentally change from being judgmental to being accepting: to actively strive to better understand and share the feelings of others. It's recognizing that people's basic needs come before they can understand and learn from each other. The "radical" part comes in when we can express this type of empathy even when someone's lived experiences are different from our own.

Stand Up

When I was on the "ditch the drama" reality-based leadership circuit, the owner—I'll call her Cindy—and I did a speaking engagement together in New England. During this talk, someone asked her, "What do you think about diversity?" This was not part of our intended program. Cindy's response was to tell the flea-in-the-jar story that she had heard me tell many times. It goes like this:

If you were to put fleas in an uncovered glass, they'd all jump out of it. But if you put fleas in the glass and then you put a lid on it, they'll jump up and hit their bodies against whatever that barrier is until they realize it hurts, and then they stop jumping high enough to hit the lid. Once 100 percent of them are jumping just below the lid, you can remove the lid, and the fleas won't jump out of the glass. It's a concept that behavioral scientists call learned helplessness.

When I share this story, it's in reference to people who lack personal accountability. Cindy was associating diversity issues with learned helplessness. She was suggesting that people weren't being discriminated against; rather, they were imagining obstacles that no longer existed.

We were speaking in front of hundreds of people, and it was being streamed live, so I had no idea how many people were watching. I was the only Black person in the room. I knew that I could not let this go. I could not allow the reality of systemic oppression to be conveniently dismissed. In this instant, I embraced radical empathy, and I stood up for the marginalized by asking the audience, "Who put the lid on?" then continued with a soliloquy about the fact that we talk about behaviors, but we don't want to address systems or the fact that fleas are not supposed to be in glasses with lids on them. I concluded by inviting all the HR professionals listening to consider the policies and practices that they have in place that are damaging to people in certain groups.

Cindy was pissed and fired me a short time later. I knew my speaking up would put my job at risk. However, I am committed to do my best to understand others *and* to also give a voice to those who may not be present or able to share their story.

EMPATHY VERSUS SYMPATHY

Empathy and sympathy are often interchanged, but they are distinctly different methods of and abilities for interaction and communication. As we've discussed, empathy is the ability to understand the feelings, thoughts, and circumstances of another as if one has experienced those feelings, thoughts, and circumstances oneself. Empathy involves putting yourself in the other person's shoes and understanding *why* they may have these particular feelings.

To sympathize with someone, they must seem in need in some way. This is not a requirement of empathy. When we sympathize with people, our beliefs about the severity of their situation will determine the level of sympathy. For example, someone with a mosquito bite will get less sympathy than someone else who was bitten by a shark. Also, we are more likely to be sympathetic toward someone who appears to have done nothing to "earn" their misfortune. The child who falls while running toward a parent will get more sympathy than the one who was doing something that they had been specifically told not to do and has fallen as a result.

There are authors whom I respect who write about sympathy as if it is a negative. I disagree. When something awful happens to someone, I often feel sorry for them. I may even be sad or mad with them. While it is important to sympathize with other people's misfortune, this is not what empathy is, and the distinction matters. Sympathy is not a bad thing.

CHIPPING TOWARD UNDERSTANDING

I have come to understand the concept of empathy the hard way—not only consequences of my own unempathetic behavior, some of which I have shared, but also the unempathetic responses from others and how that felt for me. Here are a couple of firsthand experiences that inched me closer to my empathetic journey.

When I worked as an operations manager for a printing company, I had a great boss, Ed. Why did I think he was great? Because he supported my autonomy as a manager and allowed me to push back on the "it's the way we've always done it" mentality. He was also a genuinely nice guy, always ready with a "good morning" or asking if I wanted to grab lunch together or maybe go for a run. It was a positive relationship.

In 2009, while I was going through a painful divorce, my stepdad died. Ed knew I had often been coming to the facility at three in the morning, working with the third shift. He knew that I was there at that ungodly hour far more than anyone with a family should be. Yet when I told Ed about my stepfather, he made it a point to let me know that the bereavement policy was for immediate family (which was extremely limited and did not include "step" anything), and so therefore I would need to use my vacation days.

After I had been back a few weeks, Ed casually asked, "Hey, how are you doing today?"

To which I replied, "You know, Ed, it's been like seven days since I cried. So, I think I'm good." Ed did not know what to do with that information. He looked shocked and visibly confused, and so he did nothing. He did not try to acknowledge that I was struggling or empathize with or support me during this painful time in my life. I was shocked as well. Almost all the leaders in our organization were graduates of the emotionally intelligent leadership course. They all were taught to behave as if they cared. In the moment, he saw me as such a hard-nosed leader that he couldn't even imagine that I had emotions to be intelligent about. I wouldn't say this experience was a catalyst for my empathy awareness, but it was another little chipping away to make me think, "Well, shit, I just lost my dad, my second marriage has fallen apart, of course I'm crying. What would cause people to miss that?"

Time and my newly developed empathy muscle have provided me perspective on the how and why Ed responded the way he did. Let's first talk about Ed's surprise that I had been crying. At that time, my nickname at the company was the Nickinator—a combination of *Nicole* and *terminator*. It was a nickname I was proud of. I got results without any care or concern for the people who got in my way. When I showed up, people were afraid, and I loved it.

Knowing this about me, *you* are probably now empathizing with Ed's inability to understand that I was a person with feelings, and that yes, even the Nickinator cried sometimes. I can now empathize with *his* position as well.

Today, I am keenly aware of the path that would lead Ed to inform me that I couldn't use bereavement leave to grieve the loss of my stepdad. An engineer's job is to think and make decisions objectively and logically. It is logical and reasonable from an engineering perspective for processes to be uniform. Doing so drives costs down and quality up and reduces error. Operating from that lens only, a lens of listening for accuracy rather than listening for understanding, I understand why he felt the need to inform me of the policy and that

I needed to follow it. Honestly, at that time, I'm not sure I would have responded any differently had I been in Ed's shoes.

I now perceive standard bereavement leave and other policy-over-people practices in a whole new light, which I'll share with you when we delve into who benefits from empathy.

LISTENING FOR UNDERSTANDING

Stacey Watson, during the time she was my therapist, got me unstuck from my rational, fact-driven engineer brain long enough to grasp how I could, in fact, practice empathy. I'm a person who needs accuracy to understand what someone is saying. For a technical person, especially a chemical engineer, accuracy can mean the difference between life and death. If I get this wrong, there might be a little too much chlorine in your water, a little too much of the active ingredient in your medicine, the bomb might not go off exactly when it should. Accurate is what we are trained to be, and it is what I saw as my greatest towering strength.

When I told my therapist that when people give me the facts, I get what they're saying, and that if their details and facts and my details and facts don't line up, I'm lost. She said, "Oh, no, that's not how empathy works. If you want to understand where a person is coming from, you need to listen for understanding, not accuracy." When you listen for understanding, you work from the other person's set of facts even if, to you, they are not right.

A common example of helping people move from listening for facts to listening for understanding can be found in Stacey's work with couples.

Sometimes even in counseling, people will get stuck in the facts and need help to move to understanding. This happens often with couples, and it goes something like this:

Partner one: "We never spend time together. I'm feeling disconnected ... "

Partner two interrupts: "That's not true. Last week we went out to dinner, two weeks ago we went to the cookout at your mom's, and the week before that, we met up with Jane and Joe for drinks."

While everything partner two said is factual—they did spend time together three times over the past three weeks—they are not solving partner one's feeling of disconnect. My role is to acknowledge that while partner two is right—those facts are indeed true—they are not matching with partner one's need for connection. One person is talking about dates and times, and the other person is talking about doing things that makes them feel connected. Partner two must commit to listening for understanding to decide whether three times wasn't frequent enough to create connectedness for their partner or maybe those three activities weren't the kind of connection their partner was looking for.

This example was a pivotal moment for me. The facts are the facts. However, we can choose to be right, or we can choose to get it right. Focusing on the facts and accuracy of statements can cause us to get it wrong at times. This is not how a trained scientist thinks. It was my realization that people are not processes to be solved and that the skills I pride myself on as an engineer do not necessarily translate to human-to-human communications that are not process based. I continue to work hard to hone my skill of listening for understanding, and I notice my progress.

> **People are not processes to be solved.**

Recently, I was at a conference for CEOs in North Carolina, and after I gave my presentation, this enthusiastic gentleman came over to speak with me. He told me how great he thought my presentation was and about how he worked with "colored people" back home and how impressed he was with how "articulate" I was. If this gentleman had approached me like this three or four years ago, I would have ripped him apart for his total and utter ignorance and offensiveness. But I am an empathetic work in progress, and although in my head I was like, "What in the world?!?" I took a breath and listened for understanding, not for accuracy.

Understanding #1: This CEO was genuinely excited to speak with me about my presentation and wanted to learn more.

Understanding #2: This individual gave no sign that he *intended* to offend me.

Understanding #3: If this individual grew up in a rural area, with limited exposure to people who were not white, like him, and that is all he had known, he may not understand that saying "colored people" and "people of color" are not one and the same. Therefore, he may not understand the offense.

Now, I want to make perfectly clear that my listening for understanding does *not* mean that I should not address his ignorance and offensiveness; it just means that I need to do so with empathy. It is in these moments that I draw on the wise words of Dr. Roberts: "Nicole, do you want to be right, or do you want to be effective?" I'm not going to lie; I do still want to be right most of the time, but I also understand that there are circumstances when it is more important to be effective. This was one of those circumstances.

Had I jumped on my first "What in the world?" thought, I would have instantly alienated him, and what would that have solved? I'd walk away irritated, and he would walk away still ignorant. So, we engaged in conversation and built a rapport that led to an opportunity for me to explain, in a way that he could productively process, why most Black people would find his terminology offensive.

When I am shocked by anything another person does, it is a sign that I need to lean in to empathy. Let's assume no one is in danger and we have time and space to engage in empathetic listening. In this case, both were true. I asked him questions as if he were using the sensitive language. These were the questions I would typically ask a person excited to talk after a session.

What have you done related to leadership training on the topic thus far?

How can we be helpful?

I listened to his answers, and he had done some incredible work already and wanted to continue the work with my firm. I listened more and smiled, as I always do. Then, before he walked away, I asked him to work on something for me—use the term "people of color." Without pause, he said absolutely!

I know all exchanges won't be that easy or simple, but how many more conversations could be more effective if we started with empathetic listening?

EMPATHY CAN BE HARD

Sometimes it's hard to have empathy. Empathy requires experience, and until we've walked in another person's shoes, we may find it difficult or impossible to understand the emotions they are experiencing or why they do the things they do. It isn't fair to judge others based on our own experiences, but we do it all the time. Often we don't even realize it. This is not because we are bad people. It may be that we simply haven't developed empathy yet, or maybe we do practice empathy, but we've fallen into an empathy trap.

The truth is, whether you are born with a tendency to be empathetic or you consciously practice empathy daily, we are all what I call evolving empathizers. Empathy is imperfect, and we never arrive at a final empathizing destination where we can go, "Got it. I don't even need to pay attention anymore, because I empathize with everyone in every situation that I meet." That's never going to happen, because (1) if we felt all the feelings of everyone around us all the time, we'd be too drained to ever get out of bed in the morning, and (2) life experiences constantly expand and change our perspectives and the perspectives of others, and we can't understand those changing perspectives without continual effort and awareness.

So, how do you overcome empathy traps? By awareness of what they are and attention to when you are prone to them—trust me, no one is immune. Take a moment to review the empathizer traps below and honestly acknowledge ones that you have fallen into and how you can do better, and don't forget to celebrate the ones you've overcome.

Stingy Empathizer: The stingy empathizer chooses who is and isn't worthy of their empathy. We all can easily fall into this trap without realizing it, especially when it's a perspective or situation that is drastically different from our own. Someone who has never lost a job or who has never had to face a difficult challenge on their own may perceive someone who is living on the street and begging for money as someone who is lazy and unwilling to work and has no one to blame but themselves for their situation.

But if you believe that each of us has the same inherent worth, that we are deserving of the same dignity that we each believe we deserve ourselves, then you will believe that everyone is worthy of empathy. In that mindset, you will be able to recognize the person who is homeless as an individual—a son, daughter, sister, uncle, mother, father, veteran, artist, athlete, teacher, firefighter—who lost their way. They made some bad decisions along the way—who hasn't? Or some bad decisions were made for them. Maybe they were laid off, and before they could find another job, they fell behind on their rent and were evicted. It's damn near impossible to look for employment when you have no place to live, because your days are consumed with where you will sleep each night, how you will find food, clothing, and bathroom and shower facilities. Now, imagine having no support network to help you in that situation.

I can imagine. There have been several times in my life when my network was instrumental to me. When I started my consulting business, I was afraid because I thought the move represented a lack of stability. One of my friends asked me what was the worst that could happen. I went through almost all the worst-case scenarios. Based on the people I know and the access I have, I could end up being homeless, but for me that wouldn't mean living on the streets. I am privileged enough to have family and friends who would allow me to live with them for a little while. Everyone doesn't have this access, and it often has nothing to do with personal choices. My friend's question gave me the courage I needed to take a bold step. And then because he remembered what he thought and felt when he started his firm, he took this intellectual exercise a step forward. He offered to meet my basic financial needs any month I couldn't afford to pay myself. I never needed him to make good on that promise, but knowing he understood my challenges and supported me was empowering. He was the antithesis of stingy.

We need to stop being stingy with our willingness to understand another human being. We have all sought empathy in our lives. Any time you have asked another person to listen to your story and understand what you are going through, you have sought and, hopefully, received empathy. If we all seek it, shouldn't we all offer it as well?

Reluctant Empathizer: The reluctant empathizer is someone who has developed their empathy muscle and puts it into practice but who on occasion finds themselves holding their empathy back. Unlike the stingy empathizer, it is not because they don't think the individual or group is deserving; rather, it is based on concern for the consequences of displaying their empathy. When the idea that empathy equals weakness is so prevalent in our society, it can be easier to sit on the sidelines and withhold your empathy than to risk being perceived as weak or unaligned with the majority.

If you've ever been bullied and your friends watched from the sidelines and then empathized with you in private, or you've been the friend who stood on the sidelines, you know what I am talking about. And this isn't just playground stuff. It happens all the time in the work environment and in public and social settings. The desire to empathize is there, but instead we choose to turn away.

We need to stop holding back our empathy for fear of how we will be perceived. When we display our empathy unapologetically and with confidence, others will begin to perceive it as the incredibly beneficial strength that it is.

Impatient Empathizer: Impatient empathizers listen for understanding, and they empathize with the person they are listening to, but once the exchange has happened, they want the other person to move on already. Empathy just doesn't work that way. Empathy includes supporting a person through the time and space they need to work through their feelings or circumstance.

This impatient form of empathy often occurs when we have experienced a significant loss and everyone around us is ready to move on. The funeral is over, the sympathy cards and flowers have been sent and homecooked meals delivered, so why aren't you back to work, school, life as usual? When we find ourselves unable to understand, to empathize with why someone continues to feel the way they do, we do have another choice: we offer grace and kindness instead of pushing them to get over it or move forward before they are ready.

Natural Empathizer: Some people are born with an already developed empathy muscle that enables them to empathize without having to think about it. I am not one of those people. I've had to be hit over the head multiple times to understand empathy for the strength that it is and to develop my willingness to embrace it. One benefit of my learned perspective is my objective view of empathy, and what I've realized is that natural empathizers have empathy traps too.

Natural empathizers can fall into the trap of thinking they don't need to work their empathy muscle, that they don't need to pay attention to how they empathize (are they, at times, being reluctant or stingy?). They may not understand that we are all evolving empathizers who must continue to strengthen our empathy muscles.

I have also experienced natural empathizers who believe the myth that you're either born with it or you're not, and they set themselves above those who have not come to empathy naturally and don't believe they have the potential to be empathetic.

I think the traps that natural empathizers fall into are true for anyone with a natural skill or talent. The key is to recognize the potential traps and do the work to avoid them.

Judging Empathizer: The judging empathizer judges those of us who may not always be on top of our empathy game. In those instances, judging empathizers may not say it (and sometimes they have), but they are certainly thinking, "What is wrong with you? How can you be so unempathetic?"

Rather than judging another's lack of empathy in that moment, take the opportunity to be a nurturing empathizer by helping and encouraging others to develop their own empathy muscle.

Nurturing Empathizer: The nurturing empathizer does not fall into any of the empathy traps. It is an empathizer state that we should all aspire to. They are the empathizers who are willing to help others on their empathy journey.

Read through the list again and be honest about all the traps you have fallen into. Think about those scenarios and ask yourself, "If I had provided empathy in that situation, what would that have looked like? Who would have benefited from my empathy? How would I have benefited?" I know that I have said this more than once, but it is critical to understand and acknowledge that you have sought empathy at varying points in your life, whether you realize it or not. Any time you have asked someone to understand your dilemma, choice, experience, feeling, values, you have sought empathy. How did you feel when you knew the person understood where you were coming from or perhaps where you were going to?

I love the Leslie Jamison description of empathy as a kind of travel. "Empathy requires us to be a respectful guest who is there to observe, reflect, and seek to understand another person's experience."[8] To be able to develop the ability to feel another's experience, we must extend ourselves to travel across our borders and into someone else's experiences, allowing us to peer into someone else's feelings, thoughts, and ideas to find where they intersect with our own.

---

8   Leslie Jamison, "What Is Empathy?" Journal of Social and Emotional Learning, October 2020, https://www.crslearn.org/publication/the-power-of-empathy/.

Chapter 4

Who Benefits? Yes, You!

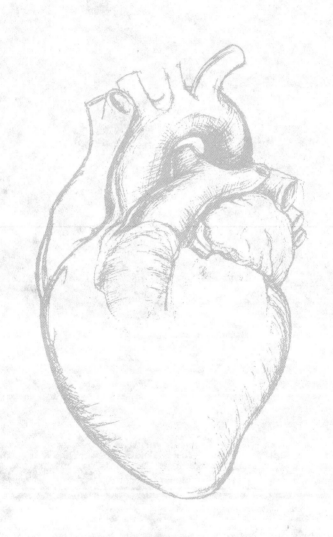

Who looks outside, dreams; who looks inside, awakes.

—CARL JUNG

While I won't bog you down with the scientific details, I will, for my logical, rational non–empathy seekers, begin by sharing basic scientific research that proves the very real benefits of empathy.

Let's start with empathy and its impact on health outcomes. In a 2011 study of 891 diabetic patients treated by twenty-nine family physicians over a four-year period, the physicians who had high empathy scores had better patient outcomes. Fifty-six percent of their patients with diabetes had good control of their A1c levels, versus 40 percent of the patients of their less empathetic colleagues. Their patients also had better good cholesterol (LDL-C) levels than their lower-empathy-scoring colleagues—59 percent versus 44 percent. The study's findings concluded that a positive relationship between a physician's empathy and patients' clinical outcomes does exist.[9]

The health benefits of empathy are not related just to diabetes and heart health. Through the research and review of pilot and retention studies, a randomized controlled trial, and a large-scale observational study, Helen Riess, associate professor of psychiatry at Harvard Medical School and director of the Empathy and Relational Science

---

9   Mohammadreza Hojat, Daniel Z Louis, Fred W Markham, Richard Wender, Carol Rabinowitz, Joseph S Gonnella, "Physicians' empathy and clinical outcomes for diabetic patients," accessed: September 19, 2022, pubmed.ncbi.nlm.nih.gov, https://pubmed.ncbi.nlm.nih.gov/21248604/.

Program at Massachusetts General Hospital in Boston, concluded that empathetic medical care is associated with many benefits, including improved

- patient experiences

- patient compliance with treatment recommendations

- clinical outcomes

- physician retention

as well as a decrease in medical errors and malpractice claims.[10]

What about the impact of empathy on education?

A 2017 study by faculty at the Leiden University and the Leiden Institute for Brain and Cognition in Leiden, Netherlands, showed the following:

- Children with higher levels of empathy are better able to regulate their emotions, show less aggression, and act in a more prosocial way.

- Higher affective empathy predicts constructive conflict resolution when encountering problems with friends.

- Cognitive empathy predicts higher-quality friendships involving mutual reciprocity and stability.

- Overall, empathy is important for bonding with primary caregivers, friends, and other eminent people.

---

10   Sandy Overgaauw, Carolien Rieffe, Evelien Broekhof, Eveline A. Crone, Berna Guroglu, "Assessing Empathy across Childhood and Adolescence: Validation of the Empathy Questionnaire for Children and Adolescents," frontiersin.org, May 29, 2017,https://www.frontiersin.org/articles/10.3389/fpsyg.2017.00870/full.

- The lack of empathy has also been related to the development of problem behaviors. Interestingly, cognitive empathy without the affective or emotional part is related to higher levels of bullying. Children need to develop both.

In *Belonging through a Culture of Dignity*, Dr. Floyd Cobb and John Krownapple state, "The research on empathy should wake us up like a shot of espresso." Why? Because, while we know that relationships make a difference in a child's educational experience, the quality of that teacher-student relationship can be improved based on the teacher's ability for empathy. The outcomes of heightened empathetic teacher-student relationships resulted in accelerated growth and achievement equal to 1.5 years of growth per one year of classroom time.

In one study, teachers took part in fourteen days of empathy strength training, which included reading about empathy and discussing the importance of keeping positive relationships with children who misbehave. The trained group of teachers were half as likely to suspend students over the course of a school year than their colleagues who did not receive the training. Take a moment to think of the lifetime impact on both sets of students.[11]

While the research shows us the value of empathy in numbers, we know that those numbers represent people. Nonetheless, it can still be difficult to put a face to the data and genuinely appreciate the human impact and put a face to the numbers.

I'm going to let my colleague Dr. Ian Roberts provide you those faces by starting at the beginning with a gift of empathy that Dr. Roberts received as a young man and the profound impact that gift had on his life.

---

11   Belonging Through a Culture of Dignity, Floyd Cobb and John Krownapple, November 12, 2019.

In high school, Dr. Roberts used to fight all the time. He likes to say he had a "proclivity to use his hands and fists to resolve problems," but the big words don't dignify his behavior. His high school principal, Mrs. Alexander, knew him well. She had given him many chances during this period in his life, but the last incident during his senior year involved the police! She'd had it and decided his chances had run out. She typed up his expulsion letter as he sat on the other side of her desk watching. She then printed one copy to go home to his mother and one to go to the school board.

In that moment, I wasn't concerned about the letter going to the school board. The copy going to my mom, that was a whole different story. I could not let that happen, and so I decided this was my time to beg. I knew my offenses were egregious enough to justify Mrs. Alexander kicking me out of school, but I pleaded with her not to. Fortunately for me, she understood what was at stake for me and offered me one final chance. The chance had tough parameters for me. They included me coming to her office every morning at 7:00, even though school started at 8:45. I was a student athlete. I was the person who all my friends wanted to pick up at home in the morning or walk to school with. Deciding to agree to arrive at her office at seven every morning would significantly change my social calendar, and it would do so for the entire second half of my senior year.

Mrs. Alexander told the young Ian that if he missed one day or if he showed up to her office at 7:01 a.m., he shouldn't bother to knock on her door, because she was going to look at the clock, get up, and put his expulsion letter express mail to the board and to his mom. He chose to miss out on those social opportunities with his friends and show up to this woman's office at seven every morning rather than be expelled.

> *I got there every single day on time. There were times I was racing toward her office because I was determined not to get there at 7:01. Every morning, Mrs. Alexander did three things: First she would start by asking me about my homework and made sure that I'd done it. Second, she'd have me file some papers and do some work around the office. And third, every day before I left—I'll never forget this—she would pull her blinds down, because she didn't want anyone to see her praying with me, and she would hold out her hand to me, and I would reluctantly give her my hand. She would place her other hand on my forehead, and she would say these long prayers. I graduated salutatorian of my class.*

> *It wasn't until many years later that I realized how life changing that chance Mrs. Alexander gave me was. I had an epiphany more than a decade after graduation, when I qualified as an Olympic athlete, and I received sponsorship to take someone with me to the games in Australia, including round-trip airfare and front seats at the stadium in Sydney, and I asked my mom, who is not an enthusiastic traveler, to come with me. She told me absolutely not; she's not traveling around the world, and she would support me from her living room.*

> *In the moment, I flashed back on my principal, and I thought to myself, What if she had not put away those expulsion papers? What if she had not given me one more chance? Would I have been able to matriculate through some of the most prestigious universities in the world and ultimately get into the pinnacle of athletics, the Olympic Games? I hadn't seen Mrs. Alexander*

since she shook my hand and handed me my high school diploma
many moons ago, and when I reached out to find her, I learned
she had passed away a couple of years before.

While on his way to compete on the biggest stage of the world, Ian realized that his experience with Mrs. Alexander had sparked his empathetic journey. He realized not only did Mrs. Alexander make the time and effort to understand, but she also chose to act with no expectation of reciprocity. She just did it.

I believe every person on this earth has had an experience where
they were the beneficiary of empathy. And if only we can go
back into that place to be introspective and think about what
that moment was, how that moment felt, we'll be inspired to
grow our own empathy muscles. Mrs. Alexander provided me
that moment. The moment that made me want to develop my
empathy muscle. I remain committed to spending the rest of
my life allowing those with whom I come into contact to be
beneficiaries of empathy and for me to be a giver of it.

Dr. Roberts is undeniably an empathetic leader, gifting empathy to colleagues and students without judgment and without expectation of reciprocity. He is one reason I committed to my empathy journey and the reason I have come so far. He is also the epitome of the power of empathy's ripple effect. The gift he was bestowed by Mrs. Alexander has been replicated countless times, the impact immeasurable. Let me share with you one story (of many) that shows the profound impact of Dr. Roberts's decision to lead with empathy.

Dawn was a senior at the high school where Dr. Roberts was principal. She was an outstanding student. One morning in her AP English class, Dawn put her head on the desk to sleep. The teacher touched her on the shoulder, awakening her, and said, "You know, you can't sleep in my class." The teacher continued to teach, and Dawn put her head back on the desk. The teacher came around a second time and tapped Dawn on her shoulder, telling her to wake up. The third time the teacher came around to tap Dawn on the shoulder, Dawn angrily stood up and pushed the teacher. The teacher tripped over a desk, fell, and hit her head, resulting in an emergency call being made to the school police and Dr. Roberts.

When they all arrived at the classroom, the teacher was sitting, crying, holding her head. Dawn was escorted to Dr. Roberts's office. His school and the school district had a zero tolerance policy for any student who assaulted a teacher. It's an unforgivable offense, and the student is immediately expelled. The situation baffled Dr. Roberts because Dawn was an honor roll student, and she hadn't had a single discipline infraction in four years, not even one. Through her tears, Dawn disclosed that she had not gotten any rest the night before because she was forced to perform sex acts on multiple men so that her mother could get the heroin she needed to feed her addiction.

I want you to take a moment to take that in. A young woman who is being sexually assaulted at home on a regular basis is about to be expelled from school because the school has a zero tolerance policy, regardless of circumstances—a policy with no exceptions for what people are going through.[12] I'll let Dr. Roberts share the rest of the story.

---

12 Zero tolerance policies, which became popular in the 1980s and continue to be widely implemented today, are devoid of empathy and have proven to have significant negative implications. According to the American Psychological Association, zero tolerance policies do not consider children's lapses in judgment or developmental immaturity as a normal aspect of development, nor do they consider that the behavior is not occurring because the child intends to do harm. These policies may exacerbate the normal challenges of adolescence and enforce severe punishments that are not warranted. Evidence indicates that referrals to the juvenile justice system for infractions once handled in the schools have increased. 2006, apa.org (https://www.apa.org/news/press/releases/2006/08/zero-tolerance)

My immediate reaction after hearing what was happening to Dawn was to call our social worker into the office. The three of us sat down, and Dawn shared more of her story—one that had been going on for two years. I asked Dawn, "Why didn't you leave home if this was happening?"

"Well, Dr. Roberts," she said, "You know how you had given me permission earlier this year to get to school late sometimes because I had to take my baby sister to school?"

"Yes," I said.

"The reason I did not leave is because I just knew that if I did, my mom would do this to my baby sister because my mom is just an addict."

Dawn had endured the unimaginable, and I did not care what the superintendent's policy, the school board's policy, or the school district's policies were. I made the decision that Dawn would not be suspended, much less be expelled. We referred her to social services, and I remained committed to making sure she graduated from school.

Because I made a decision that put Dawn above policy, 100 percent of the teachers and staff in that building, about 126 people, stopped talking to me. They rolled their eyes when they passed me in the hall; they left notes under my door, "How dare you allow this kind of environment where a teacher can be assaulted?" This went on for almost two weeks until, unfortunately, the word got out about Dawn being placed with social services and what she had endured. The attitudes of the staff quickly changed, and I came into my office one day to find flowers and chocolates and notes of apology for their actions and gratitude for mine.

Oftentimes when you make empathy-based decisions, everyone is not likely to agree with them, especially if they don't have context. I believe it's important to remain true to who we say we are going to be for our children. Dawn did graduate from high school and received a full ride to attend undergrad at a university in Pennsylvania. Eventually, she finished graduate school and became a social worker. It was a truly profound experience.

Dawn's story is an exceptional one. In our day-to-day lives, most of us are not called upon to offer that level of empathy or push back on the policies that allow no exceptions. But there are everyday instances when we can practice empathy, and in doing so, you will find that the practice serves not only the person you offer it to but also you, the giver.

NEXT IN LINE, PLEASE

We've all been in the checkout line at the grocery store and the person in front of us is moving so incredibly slowly that we have all we can do to stifle the scream rising inside us. We can't allow our scream to escape, but that doesn't keep us from showing our annoyance. We roll our eyes and sigh loud enough for others to hear—actions we all know are super helpful, right? Will those actions make us feel better? Don't think so. Will those actions make the person in front of us move faster? Probably not. So, if we can't control how quickly the person in front of us moves, how can we choose to make this situation better? We can practice empathy.

What if instead of giving in to annoyance, we took a breath, thought about why this person was slower than what we considered acceptable—maybe this is their only social interaction all week, or maybe they have physical or mental realities that slow them down—and who says everyone must run at our designated speed anyway? When we try to find ways to understand what is going on for the other person, we may find ways to aid rather than annoy—not in an angry "helpful" way but in an understanding way. What would that experience look like for you? How would you feel when you walked out the door? Fairly good, I'm guessing. Yes, you may still be late, but being late and happy is better than being late and pissed off, both for you and the people you meet during the rest of your day.

The person you chose to help or not to stress out with your exasperation is going to leave the store in a better frame of mind. You will feel better too. Everyone benefits from this empathetic exchange.

Practicing empathy throughout our day requires a conscious effort to pay attention to our own reflexive reactions and the reflexive reactions of those around us. Imagine you're in sales and you're required to hand in monthly expense reports to Susie in accounting. You enter Susie's office with a smile and say, "Here you go," as you place your monthly expense report on top of one of the piles on her desk. Susie glares at you without a word, and you think, "What's her problem?" If you take a moment to acknowledge that the report you just handed her is three days late and that last month you handed it in four days late, and the month before that … you might have a better understanding of why Susie is frustrated with you, and with that understanding, you can change the behavior that is contributing to Susie's frustration. That's powerful. Choosing to behave (handing your reports in on time) from a place of understanding, you no longer need to feel guilt or shame for constantly being late and adding stress to Susie, and you eliminate that stress and frustration that Susie was feeling. You and Susie benefit from this empathetic exchange.

Now if Susie glares at the person who turns in their report late for the first time in three years, Susie needs to take a step back, acknowledge that this is out of character for this person, check in with them to determine whether everything is okay, and listen from a place of understanding.

We all can practice empathy multiple times throughout our day. If we can begin to practice it in these small ways, together we'll begin to practice it in big ways.

BUT EMPATHY WON'T GET THE JOB DONE— OR WILL IT?

Marsha, an administrator who I worked with, was responsible for all things that informed us about who was supposed to do what and how many pieces and parts we had to have out every day. Without Marsha, I could not do my job effectively. She and I talked multiple times a day about work and only about work because that's what I cared about. While I asked, "How are you?" I usually expected the typical, "Fine." I didn't *really* expect a different or more involved answer. Marsha was introverted, which made dismissing the need to know her personally even easier. She wasn't interested in initiating the conversation.

One day when I was practicing, on HR's recommendation, trying to get to know people, I sat and talked to Marsha. You know what I found out about the person I depended on to get my job done? She had been coming to work for months wearing a catheter strapped to her abdomen while going through cancer treatment. How did I not know that a woman who I regularly interacted with was fighting for her life? I don't even know how to explain how that shifted my view of this woman, because I don't know that I would have kept coming to work through all of that. Understanding her experience gave me a greater amount of appreciation and respect for her, bringing us to a whole new level of collaboration.

If people are coming to work even though they are experiencing significant personal challenges, there's a high level of care that they have for the mission, for you, or for the work they are doing. That's important for leaders to know. Understanding where people are, what they're going through, what keeps them going, is good for you, it's good for that person, it's good for the business, it's good for everyone. Lack of understanding about who your people are is a weakness.

A gentleman I worked with for several years, Rodney, always showed up like he was mad at the world. Before you judge him, I used to appreciate Rodney's demeanor. He was like my bulldog, helping me to put the squeeze on clients and vendors when I needed a little … muscle. He had been grumbling about wanting to retire for years, but because he was a subject matter expert, his retirement would not have been beneficial to the company, so everyone kept pressuring him to stay—for ten more years! I didn't learn until just before he retired that the reason he wanted to retire was because he was concerned about his health and how much more time he was going to have with his grandkids. I worked alongside this man for years, and I never even bothered to understand who he was or why he was always so mad—I cared only about his role in helping get the job done. This is unfortunate. I can do better.

We can do better.

We need to appreciate the Marshas and provide them the support they need. We need to understand why the Rodneys want to retire and help them find a solution because it's the right thing to do and it benefits us all, including the bottom line. There is no way to factually know how my listening a little better and paying attention to people would have changed past scenarios, but I do know that there is no way my offering of empathy would have made it worse.

Leading with empathy requires companies to put people over policy, as Dr. Roberts did in his decision to put Dawn above the school's zero tolerance policy. This can be hard for leadership and those they lead to wrap their heads around. It's much easier for organizations to establish rules and use them to keep everything nice, neat, and uniform, and there are times that uniformity is necessary. As an example, a policy that states that all employees must wear safety glasses when using dangerous tools is prudent. But there are times when policies—like my inability to use bereavement leave when my stepdad died because he did not fit the policies category of "family"—cannot be based on a one-size-fits-all premise, because humans are not one size fits all, no matter what the tag on the bathrobe says.

While a bereavement policy can be uniform in the number of bereavement days a person is allowed before they must use other paid or unpaid leave time, a policy cannot determine who matters to me the most, whom I love, who my family is, or whose loss would most impact me. It just can't. Organizations must employ empathy and understanding if they are to recognize that policy should not be created over people and that when an existing policy no longer works for the people, it must be changed.

> **When an existing policy no longer works for the people, it must be changed.**

An empathetic organization approaches bereavement leave by asking each new employee, "Who are your people?" "Who are your people that if something happens to them, you'll need to take time off?" If you were raised by a foster parent or a stepparent, their loss may be more painful for you than that of your biological parent. The loss of your best friend may have greater impact than a sibling who hasn't been in your life for years. For some people, their dog may be included on their list. An organization cannot and should not decide who your people are. On the other side, the organization's knowing who truly is important to you helps it better understand and support you in the workplace. A supported employee is a more productive and loyal employee.

I can't think of a situation in which my having a better under-standing of the people involved didn't improve the situation. Consider a handful of situations in which you had a better understanding of another person or someone had a better understanding of you. How did it improve the situations for all involved? What drawbacks do you notice?

Chapter 5

Enough Already!
Setting Boundaries

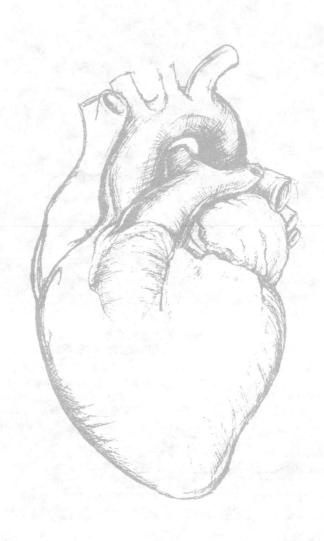

Just because you can feel their pain doesn't
mean you are supposed to carry it.

— MIND JOURNAL

You might be asking, "How am I supposed to offer others genuine and sincere understanding all the time? The answer is this: You might not be able to. And that's okay. There are many ways in which we can and should set boundaries around our empathy practice.

Dr. Roberts and I created a leadership development model called ARDAC, which stands for Awareness, Reflection, Decision, Action, and Check.

AWARENESS

REFLECTION

DECISION

ACTION

CHECK

Applying these steps to our empathy practice can help us keep building our empathy muscle while also establishing boundaries so that we don't become overwhelmed. Let's break them down.

Awareness: When you first become aware of something, it can be a beautiful thing. Maybe you have decided it's time to get in shape, and you begin working with a trainer. It's a little intimidating at first, but you discover you can do more than you thought you could. You become aware of your fitness potential, and it's exciting, and you think, "I got this." As you continue, you begin to grasp the level of commitment it takes to keep improving your fitness level *and* then maintain it. At this point, you are ready to begin the process of being healthy and getting in shape. Before the awareness entered your consciousness, it was highly unlikely that you would do anything to start the process. Awareness is the first step toward any change initiative.

> Awareness is the first step toward any change initiative.

Reflection: When you think about all that must be done, where you could be had you started sooner, and all the adjustments you must make, your awareness can morph into overwhelming feelings. When the overwhelm begins to creep in, it's time to spend some time reflecting on what has prevented you from having this awareness before. This insight might provide you with the information you need to move forward. Maybe you believed all the fitness and weight-loss ads that make it look easy, or you have a friend who doesn't seem to work too hard at it and they look like they are in great shape. Then reflect on what you want to be true about yourself in the future. This overt focus is like when you push yourself to the next fitness level and after every workout, you wake up the next morning hardly able to move because your body hurts so much. You begin to wonder if it's all worth it. But now is not the time to give up or set up boundaries.

Decision: Before you give in to the excuses for why it's not worth the effort, you must decide to commit, to recognize the value of the progress you've made so far and the benefits that it's brought you. Now, you may not be ready to run a 5K yet, but three weeks ago, you were breathing heavily simply walking around the block, and now you're walking a mile every day and it feels good, so you commit to action. You make a conscious decision about incorporating exercise into your daily routine.

Action: You determine that to reach your fitness goal, you need to start walking 1.5 miles a day, five days a week, and you need to cut some of your favorite foods from your diet. The first couple of weeks of your new routine, you're feeling good about your diet and exercise. The constant effort of thinking about what you should and shouldn't eat and how many miles you should make yourself walk each day on top of thinking about the times you haven't stuck to it is too much, and you begin to convince yourself this fitness stuff isn't so important after all. Once you act, you realize that some of your relationships are strengthened, but others are strained. Action is uncomfortable and sometimes feels unstable.

Check: You make a deliberate effort to evaluate your last four weeks. You realize that you're starting to measure progress by what you haven't done. You recognize that instead of giving yourself credit for increasing your walking to two miles a day, you have been berating yourself because you ate one of your favorite not-on-your-diet foods last week. Now is the time to recalibrate. Remind yourself of your goals. Rein yourself in on your food choices, and set some relational boundaries that work for you. An effective way to begin is to celebrate and acknowledge your wins, no matter how small. Make sure you give yourself permission to take time off from your fitness goals—even professional athletes make sure they take time to rest.

Rest is rejuvenating.

Practicing empathy works in the same way. You notice when you receive empathy as well as start to find opportunities throughout your day when you can provide empathy. Awareness of the endless opportunities for empathy can grow to the point of overwhelm. The experiences people have shared with you may be swirling around your mind, and you can't seem to let them go. Much like the initial workout struggles, this is not the time to give in. It's time to reflect on what prevented you from being aware of the opportunities to empathize with those around you to begin with and then decide to commit to continuing your empathy efforts.

For me, committing meant continuously reminding myself that there wasn't a time when I received empathy that it wasn't beneficial and that I believe I am deserving of empathy. If that is true and I also believe everyone deserves dignity, they must also deserve my under-standing. I continued with my empathy practice until I realized I was beating up on myself every time I felt I had screwed up: when I listened half-heartedly or opted out of empathizing when I had the chance because I just didn't want to take the time. What I had forgotten to do was celebrate all the times that I did offer empathy and saw the benefit for the other person and myself.

> And it's important to remind ourselves that empathy is not about solving a problem, agreeing with the other person, or trying to convince the other person to agree with you.

By checking in, I was able to adjust my mindset and begin to focus on and celebrate the times I got it right. There was another aspect of my practice that I needed to check myself—developing this idea that empathy equated to needing to "fix" people's problems. It can be an easy trap to fall into, and it's important to remind ourselves that empathy is not about solving a problem, agreeing with the other person, or trying to convince the other person to agree with you. If someone is asking for you to help, that's a different story. But if they are simply looking for you to understand, then do just that.

THE COST OF EMPATHY

We would be lying to ourselves if we said that the sharing of difficult or negative emotions is easy. The truth is it's hard, because in empathizing with another, we are, on some level, truly feeling their pain, and we have the science to prove it. Today, neuroscientists can explore the brain circuitry through functional magnetic resonance imaging in ways that they never could before. Through this technology, studies have been conducted on pain-related empathy.

Married couples were studied to ascertain what brain networks were activated when a painful stimulus was applied to the hand of one partner while the other partner could see and hear their reaction. It was discovered that the pain networks associated with emotional qualities activated the same way in both the person receiving the physical pain and the person seeing and hearing their partner in physical pain. While the observing partner could not physically feel the other's pain, they were able to emotionally feel their pain *with* them. Psychologists caution that feeling *with* another is an important distinction and serves to remind us that the emotion we may resonate with belongs to the other person and is not our own.[13]

Grief is a common feeling that is shared with others. When someone is sharing their grief with you and you are listening for understanding, the conversation *should* be focused on them. While thoughts of your own grief-related circumstances may bubble up and bring you to a higher level of understanding, it's important to remember that empathy is about feeling and honoring the other person's emotions. Your emotional experiences with grief may help you connect, but this

---

13   Trisha Dowling, "Compassion does not fatigue!" ncbi.nlm.nih.gov, July 2019, https://www.ncbi.nlm.nih.gov/pmc/articles/PMC6005077/.

is not the time to share your story. You can show up authentically for the other person. However, you must establish boundaries. This can help prevent you from feeling overwhelmed and distressed in ways that can lead to empathy fatigue and psychic numbing.

EMPATHY FATIGUE

Empathy fatigue describes the strain and exhaustion that occurs when we are exposed to the pain of others on a continual basis. This is most often prevalent in the caregiving professions. Nurses, therapists, and first responders are just a few examples of care providers who may experience mental, physical, and emotional strains because of repeatedly listening, empathizing, and assisting clients in processing their experiences and helping them manage their mental and physical health. Care providers who have experienced their own trauma may also struggle with the involuntary revisiting of their personal traumatic experiences when helping others uncover and navigate their trauma. This is called secondary trauma. Empathy and compassion fatigue can desensitize caregivers to the needs and experiences of their patients, which can result in lower-quality care, an increase in medical errors, and higher rates of anxiety and depression in the caregivers.

Caregivers need leaders who understand this phenomenon and create a culture that supports their staff with ways to establish boundaries and engage in self-care. But for now, let's focus on the challenges of empathy fatigue and psychic numbing.

PSYCHIC NUMBING

If I look at the mass, I will never act.
If I look at the one, I will.

—MOTHER TERESA

When we look at the world in numbers and think of human beings as statistics, it's easy to separate ourselves from the nameless and faceless "others." Of the seventy-three million children (about twice the population of California) in the US in 2019,[14] .0001 percent were killed by gun violence. It's easy to digest .0001 percent as insignificant. But that .0001 percent represents 3,371 children—enough to fill more than 168 classrooms of twenty students. Enough to fill more than nine schools in rural communities across America.[15] So, who is okay with their child being the .0001 percent?—because somebody's kids will be. When the percentage is low enough or the numbers high enough, psychic numbing and dangerous indifference take hold.

In 1986, the world couldn't tear their eyes away from the two-and-a-half-day rescue of eighteen-month-old Jessica McClure from an abandoned well. The saving of one child was watched and celebrated by the world. How many Americans showed this level of concern for the ninety-three school shootings in 2019? My guess is most of us aren't even aware that there were ninety-three school shootings in 2019. It becomes too much to comprehend, and we shut ourselves off. This psychic numbing breeds apathy and inaction.

---

14   https://www.childstats.gov/americaschildren/tables/pop1.asp

15   https://www.childrensdefense.org/state-of-americas-children/
soac-2021-gun-violence/

Dr. Paul Slovic explains that if we are told there are ninety-nine people in danger, and then we learn that there are one hundred people in danger, we stop feeling any difference about that one additional endangered person. And although the difference between zero people at risk and one is huge, it doesn't take much for us to feel desensitized. In a 2014 study, Dr. Slovic recorded a decrease in empathy toward children in need as soon as the number of victims increased from one to two.[16]

These phenomena can be found in the simple exercise of collecting coats for people who need them. The data would suggest that if I believe ninety-nine people need coats, I will try to organize to make that happen. The moment it becomes one hundred people who need coats, I no longer think of people in need but rather data points, and when we think of data points instead of actual humans, we begin to think that just one more doesn't matter. But if we flip it and you're one of that hundred and somebody gives you a coat, it matters to you, and the giver of the coat has in fact made a difference. Yes, there are ninety-nine more people who still do not have coats, but you have one, and you're warm today, and that matters. Recognizing the individual rather than the number or the statistic is the humanistic component to empathy that we must keep reminding ourselves to return to.

There are people at the end of data points.

—DR. IAN A. ROBERTS

---

16 Paul Slovic, "Compassion Fade: Affect and Charity Are Greatest for a Single Child in Need," PLoS One, June 18, 2014, https://journals.plos.org/plosone/article?id=10.1371/journal.pone.0100115.

FOUR HOURS ON A BEACH

Spending four hours on a beach where I was not allowed to speak or to have a phone, money, or any type of identification made me realize that I have been a stingy empathizer and that I needed to stop convincing myself that if I couldn't "fix" a person or situation that I shouldn't bother to try.

In 2015 I participated in this retreat in which I was dropped off in Malibu without any money, phone, etc. with the instructions that I was not to speak a word to anyone and that I would be picked back up in four hours. Well, if you can't talk and you don't have any money, you're not going shopping. Right. You're not going out to eat or to the movies. Your options are limited. So, I found myself just hanging out on the beach, and the people who I found connectedness with were people without a place to call home. They were the people who would look me in the eye and just ask, "Are you hungry?" If I nodded my head yes, they might say, "I have an apple. Do you want it?"

What stood out the most to me in this experience was the indifference of the people who clearly had homes to go to. None of them made eye contact with me, let alone said hello. The man I spent the most time with that day shared his stories with me. He had been married a couple of times. Said he wasn't particularly good with relationships. Remember, I can't say even a word, so I am forced to either go sit by myself or sit with and listen to others. Through our "conversation" there were so many common threads. I, too, had been divorced. He then told me that he had lost his mother and how much he missed her. My mom had been gone three years by then, so I resonated very deeply with that. When I had nowhere to go and no option but to listen, the distance between this man and me evaporated. I could no longer convince myself that I was not like him and he was not like me.

Listening and understanding are the threads that connect us. Judgment, indifference, and fear tend to overwhelm us. The latter are how we trick ourselves into thinking that someone is not equal to us, not deserving of the same things we are, not worth looking them in their eyes. We convince ourselves if there are likenesses, then the same misfortune will happen to us. We fear we will recognize the evil that we see in others in ourselves, or we slip into overwhelming feelings thinking that problem is too big for us to fix, so we may as well do nothing. I think I convinced myself of all those things when I was being a stingy empathizer.

I had a friend, Andrea, who, after her first child was born, suffered from postpartum depression. With the birth of her second child, she developed paranoid schizophrenia. Eventually, she ended up living on the street. Andrea was not an acquaintance of mine; she had been a best friend. There were three of us, Andrea, Brandy, and me, and we spent all our time together through high school. I knew what had happened to Andrea, and one day I saw her standing on the corner of the expressway ramp. In that moment of recognition, all I felt was embarrassment. I didn't even yield at the end of the ramp because all I wanted to do was get away as quickly as I could. It's one of the most shameful moments of my life.

At the end of the nine-day retreat, I shared this story with the organizer. I tried to explain why I had done that. There was part of me that worried if Andrea's mind could fail, mine could fail me too. I don't know exactly what caused me to behave that way, but I know I felt embarrassment for myself and for her, and I had chosen to ignore her. The organizer looked at me and said, "You're going to get another chance to make that right."

93

When I got back to Kansas City, I told my son about Andrea, and he was mortified. "Mom, you did what?" He could not believe that I ignored my friend. However, that same week, I was driving my son to the barbershop, the same barbershop I had been driving him to for over a decade. It was raining, and somehow, I missed my exit. I got off on the next exit, turned around, and found myself at an unfamiliar intersection. There I saw a woman standing on the corner. I didn't recognize her. She called out my name. In that moment, I realized who it was. I began shaking and told my son, "That's Andrea." I waved to her and pulled over. She came over, and we said hello, and I asked her what she needed, what would be helpful. She told me that she needed a ride somewhere, and I told her to hop in. Within seconds, she said, "I don't really need a ride. I just need fifteen dollars." I asked my son to give her the money. We pulled over again. Andrea and I got out and hugged, and she walked back into the rain.

I did not solve homelessness that day. I did not get Andrea off the street that day either. But Andrea got all my empathy and dignity that day. And who was restored? I think it was me. My experience on the beach, when I was invisible to all the people passing through, changed me. When I see someone who is homeless on the street, I look them in the eye and I say, "Hello." It is a simple humanizing gesture. If I choose to give the person money, I don't judge them for how they may spend it. Why give begrudgingly? If I choose not to give money to the individual, I don't judge them for asking me. Even my "no" can be delivered with dignity.

Just because you can't help everyone doesn't mean you can't help someone.

CIRCLE OF CONTROL VERSUS CIRCLE OF CONCERN

I share these empathy challenges because awareness is key to mitigating their effects. Being aware of the potential costs of empathy to your well-being is the important first step in setting your personal boundaries and practicing self-care. Establishing my own circle of concern works well for me. I reflect on who and what are concerns in my life. Family, friends, colleagues, caring for my family, and propelling my work forward are in my intimate circle of concern. I also have concern for gun violence, homelessness, social injustice, climate change—it's an extensive list, but I can't have impact in every aspect that I believe needs work. So, what can I do?

I establish my circle of control within my circle of concern, and I decide how I can help and impact these people and areas of concern and commit to taking action.

First things first, when I find myself becoming overwhelmed, I write down everything that I'm thinking about. Writing it on paper gives me the tangibility: something to look at, something to respond to. I put it in two distinct categories. First, I list my circle of concerns (that's that long, all-encompassing list). Then I break out over what on that list I can exert some level of control.

I accept that there are things that I cannot change in a big way, like global warming. Twenty-five years ago, people were sounding the alarm bell that this was what was going to happen, and hardly anyone would listen. So, here we are with hurricanes and forest fires and ice caps melting and all these immense things. But today I'm not in a position to offer significant impact. It's not my work. It's not even part of my volunteer opportunities. I don't even have the capacity to care deeply about that. I am concerned, but it is not in my control, so I do my small part. I set my thermostat as high as I can in the hot weather and as low as I can in the chilly weather. I drive a hybrid vehicle. I recycle. As for environmental or energy justice, I work closely with my clients who are positioned to impact change in this area.

I can't exert any more control over global warming than that when I consider what my personal values are and the mission and vision of my company. We are not environmentalists. We specialize in inclusive leadership. Conversely, when a politician throws out a dog whistle that is antiwoman or anti–people of color, it's clear to me that I need to speak up about that, regardless of the implications. My struggle is always that I want to be liked. Sometimes we don't take action in areas where we have control because we are concerned about the negative perceptions of other people. You mustn't do that. Please affect the things that you can. While I could easily pretend that politics don't fall into my circle of control, I have chosen this work, and so I act and draw on my resources and do everything I can to effect change. You must also allow your mission and vision to guide your decisions. Excuses, indifference, and fear get in the way of practicing empathy in impactful ways.

When I conduct this exercise with groups, I ask participants to create three columns: circle of concern, circle of control, and circle of influence. I go old school with this exercise and pull out a flip chart and write it so people can see it. I ask them to share everything that is on their minds. They then label each item as control, concern, or influence. They can then physically mark out things that are not in their circle of control or influence. That action alone is a stress reliever: to see the huge list shrink down to a smaller list. There are things we may not be able to control but we can influence. There are also things we can neither control nor influence. I ask the group to vote on which items to work on based on the list in their three columns, recognizing that there will always be competing priorities and not enough resources.

I ask the group to agree that if it's completely out of our control or influence, we are not going to focus our time on it. When we get things down to this much smaller list of things we control and influence, we can demonstrate personal accountability, which is nothing more than understanding that we choose our destiny, that we have the power to make things so. This understanding infuses so much energy and hope. It restores passion. It diminishes the sense of defeat we feel when we focus on things outside our control.

We can't control the weather, and so to continue to lament the weather would just be painful. What we can control is our response to the weather, how we're going to staff up or staff down when the weather changes, how we think about our industry that differs from other industries that weather doesn't impact as much. Those responses (controls) will dictate who we hire, not because we're being exclusionary but because we're trying to find people who will be happy with this kind of ambiguous work. This is the method I've developed that works for me and that I have seen success within my client groups.

One thing I'm not great at but I've seen others do, even around circle of control, is to say, "I'm going to organize with other people to address this thing that I cannot control alone." One individual person in poverty cannot truly impact policy. But if you organize people all around the country surrounding living wages, they can make progress. The Poor People's Campaign has demonstrated it. I might not know how to do that, but I continue to stretch myself on the things important to me, and launching an empathy revolution is at the top of my list, requiring me to draw on compassionate empathy and invite others (like you) to join me.

THE IMPORTANCE OF SELF-COMPASSION

Self-compassion is helpful if you find that you struggle with boundary setting or if you need added support. Rasmus Hougaard, founder and CEO of Potential Project, suggests some tips for increasing compassion in your leadership:[17]

Have more self-compassion: Having genuine compassion for others starts with having compassion for yourself. If you're overloaded and out of balance, it's impossible to help others find their balance. Self-compassion includes getting quality sleep and taking breaks during the day. For many leaders, self-compassion means letting go of obsessive self-criticism. Stop criticizing yourself for what you could have done differently or better. Instead, cultivate self-talk that is positive. Then reframe setbacks as learning experiences. What will you do differently in the future?

Check your intention: Make a habit of checking your intention before you meet others. Keeping your intentions in mind, ask yourself, How can I best be of benefit to this person or these people?

If you are engaging in gestures haphazardly, you will burn out. Your boundaries will be tested without consideration for your goals and your own intentions. Intentionality breeds wholeheartedness. Wholeheartedness is the antidote to fatigue.

---

17   Rasmus Hougaard, "Four Reasons Why Compassion Is Better For Humanity Than Empathy," forbes.com, July 8, 2020, https://www.forbes.com/sites/rasmushougaard/2020/07/08/four-reasons-why-compassion-is-better-for-humanity-than-empathy/?sh=6f02f5f7d6f9.

Chapter 6

Let's Build Your Empathy Muscle

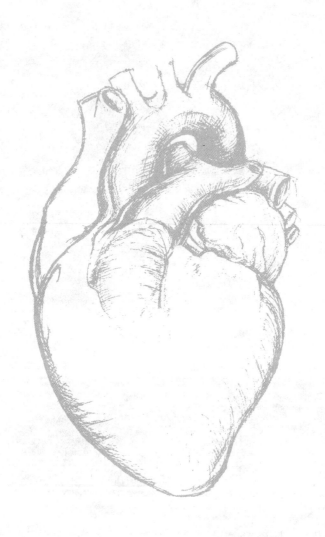

I believe empathy is the most essential
quality of civilization.

—ROGER EBERT

WHAT SPARKED
YOUR EMPATHY?

As you embark on a journey to build your empathy muscle, I encourage you to reflect on what empathy means to you. I'm not talking about the meaning in the dictionary; I'm talking about what comes to mind when you think about empathy, what has been your experience with empathy, how does empathy make you feel, what benefits and/or negative effects do you find? What form does it take in your life today? Write your thoughts down.

Now evaluate when and how your view of empathy was developed. In chapter 1, I shared with you that witnessing my mother's endless capacity to care was the genesis of my antiempathy path *and* the spark of my "let's start an empathy revolution" path. What once pushed me to step away has now helped me to find my way back. This was a significant realization for me, one that served to strengthen my resolve. It wasn't until I started this book that I ever gave any thought to why I held the beliefs I had about empathy. Once I reflected on it and realized that I had been so resistant because I didn't want to be taken advantage of, I remembered the words of my dear great-uncle Henry, "Baby, they can't use you when you give it away." Empathy is not something you decide to do for someone else. Think about your own values, and identify which ones align with empathy and which ones don't. You will find that some of your values align to empathy. Practicing empathy is a way to live out your own values.

Once you've identified the source of your views on empathy, dig a little deeper and unpack why that person, action, experience informed you the way it did. What do you still believe to be true of your initial view? How has your view changed, and why? Write your thoughts down. As you get more comfortable with the process, start the empathy conversation with others. Share what you've come to learn about your own ideas and practices of empathy, and encourage them to share theirs.

From all that you know now about empathy, do you believe you deserve to receive it? Do you believe everyone deserves to receive it? I hope the answer is yes, because if you believe that everyone deserves empathy, you also believe everyone is deserving of dignity, and that is where it all must begin.

Dignity: the quality or state of being worthy, honored, or esteemed

When you consciously look at your world, your circle of concern, for ways to offer empathy, it's important to remind yourself that not everyone has what you have. While we all have the same basic human needs (see Maslow's hierarchy of needs), we don't all have the privilege of the same level of support, health, education, or wealth to meet those needs. When you lead with that knowledge, you will understand things differently. Here's a real-life practical example to get you started.

POVERTY AND THE PARKING LOT

At times there are things that leaders don't even think about as they relate to culture. One of those things is wealth culture. This was never clearer to my team and me than when we were visiting a plant near Chicago. The employees who worked on the production floor at that plant had salaries that were greater than minimum wage, but they were still not livable wages based on the cost of living in the area. The leadership team in this facility all made over six figures.

There was a line worker who consistently violated the parking lot policy. The policy was simple: employees park in employee spots and avoid parking in spots designated for visitors. This particular employee had been warned three times. Therefore, on the fourth occurrence, the parking lot attendant supervisor towed her car. The tow fee was $250. That was the equivalent of more than two days' pay. We happened to be on site the day the car was towed. We recalled an excessive number of visitor spots, and we also noticed that the main lot was full when we drove past it to get to the visitors' parking.

Once we arrived inside, there were several leaders in the conference room discussing why employees continually violated the parking policy. Being a bit nosy, we began asking questions.

Us: Are there enough spots for employees?

First leader: Yes! (He's in the unaware destructive zone.)

Second leader: Actually, a year ago the leadership team made the decision to overlap shifts (meaning that when the third shift was leaving, the first shift was coming) in the mornings. During the overlap period, we are twelve spots short.

First leader: People should get here earlier. (Now, he's consciously destructive.)

Us: If there aren't enough spots during the change of shift, people coming early for the first shift won't solve that problem.

For this frontline worker, that $250 represented her destruction. Here's how:

- Public transportation didn't service the manufacturing facility, so without her car, she would have no way to get to work unless she used a private transportation option, which would very quickly become a financial burden.

- Every day that her car stayed in that tow lot, she would be charged an additional hundred dollars. In essence, if she didn't have $250 to fork over on day one, she would need to come up with $350 on day two.

- She couldn't take time off from work to go get her car that day because leaving her shift without asking for permission (before the day she needed the leave) would result in a write-up on her record.

- Write-ups on her record meant that she wouldn't get her quarterly bonus.

Watch what happens when you lead with understanding—you see the individual and their unique situation first and policy second. The first leadership decision to overlap the shifts created a challenge for the line workers, who, unlike management, could not adjust their arrival time to a time when there were more parking spots available. It's clear that the leaders never looked beyond their own perspectives when creating this policy.

We asked the plant manager to pay the $250 to get the woman's car out of the tow lot and to change the parking policy until they resolved the problem with the number of parking spots. For the plant manager, that $250 represented an evening hanging out with friends. For the line worker, that $250 could have resulted in the loss of her car and job and … once that cycle starts, it's incredibly difficult to stop.

Having grown up in poverty, Dr. Roberts and I both understand the culture of poverty. We could immediately see the domino effect of this policy, one that neglected to treat line workers with the same dignity afforded to their leaders, one that created a separation, a "they": Why do "they" continue to break the parking policy? Living in poverty creates its own set of challenges, and we took the opportunity to help the leaders understand that perspective by opening the leadership class that day by asking the leaders to share whether they had experienced poverty, and if they had, what were some of the things that would cause a person to be late to work.

The list included things like a flat tire, day care being closed, and utilities being shut off, making it necessary to go to another person's house to shower and get dressed. It was an extensive list. A list that the leaders who never experienced poverty had never thought of. When you have money, a flat tire is of no consequence to you because you probably have a AAA membership, can afford to rent a car, or own a secondary vehicle. When you have money, you can pay your bills, and you will not have to take a cold shower or get dressed in the dark because your utilities have been shut off. It was a revealing experience for the leaders in the room.

This organization had a mission to employ people from the community where they operated. The leadership wanted to offer people second-chance opportunities if they had arrest records, even if they had no consistent work experience. These theoretically good intentions were met with practical issues and retention challenges, not the least of which was the parking policy. To understand people requires you to step outside your bubble. We were able to help leadership do that by asking a couple of leaders to share their experience with poverty.

To their credit, the leaders in that plant ended up creating a partnership with a rideshare provider whereby they created alternative opportunities for line workers to get to and from work. They also instituted a carpool policy and sponsored a company van for employees who lived in the same areas to use in a vanpool. Some might argue that the plant leader should have also increased the level of pay for line workers. These leaders in this plant did not have that authority, but we applaud them for doing what they did have the authority to do—demonstrate empathetic leadership. Anyone at any level can start where they are and do what they can to show empathy. Where will you begin?

MASLOW'S HIERARCHY OF NEEDS

1. **Physiological Needs:** These are the essentials a human being needs for basic survival: shelter, water, food, warmth, rest, and health.

2. **Safety Needs:** We humans need to not only physically be safe but feel safe if we are to obtain the stability and security needed to progress. We must keep ourselves safe from the elements, violent conditions, and health risks. We must feel secure in our ability to provide for our and others' basic needs, such as economic security.

3. **Love and Belonging Needs:** Humans have the need to give and receive love, to feel like they belong in a group. We crave interactions through friendships, intimacy, family, and love. When deprived of these needs, individuals may experience loneliness or depression.

4. **Esteem Needs:** Esteem needs are related to a person's need to gain recognition and status and feel respected: the need for respect from others and the need for respect from oneself. Before we can hold ourselves or others in esteem, we must first believe in our/their dignity.

5. **Self-Actualization Need:** Self-actualization, the realization of an individual's full potential, is Maslow's final level in his hierarchy of needs. Once this level is reached, humans strive to become the best that they can possibly be.[18]

---

18   CFI, "Maslow's Hierarchy of Needs," corporatefinanceinstitute.com, April 21, 2022, https://corporatefinanceinstitute.com/resources/knowledge/other/maslows-hierarchy-of-needs/.

STAGES OF EVOLVING EMPATHY

When Dr. Roberts explained the process I traveled while learning to lead with empathy, he described it in four phases, the first of which was *curiosity*, in which I peppered him with questions: Why aren't you letting people who don't do their job go? How do you have the patience to keep giving them another chance? How does that even work?

The next phase was *resistance and reluctance*. Here I agreed that empathy may hold some value but felt it couldn't get you your desired outcomes. I still believed that in business, utilizing empathy could weaken an individual's or a company's ability to meet intended goals.

What Dr. Roberts calls *cautious investment* came next. During this phase, I would call Dr. Roberts, excited to share with him experiences when I had practiced empathy and it had worked! I could finally see its benefits for me, the person I offered the empathy to, and yes, even the accomplishment of outcomes. Maybe there was something to this.

Now, I was able to reach the final stage of my personal empathy evolution: *full investment*. I had witnessed the benefits and the joy of offering empathy and receiving empathy. Through this process I had become a better communicator and collaborator. I realized I could reach my goals without leaving people in my wake. I was happier. I did not move through these stages overnight; this was a multiyear evolution, and I am still a work in progress. The difference is that I now fully believe in the value of empathy. I believe that everyone is deserving of receiving empathy, everyone can give empathy, and the world is better for it. Now, I eagerly share that belief with everyone!

The watch-outs. This is my own term for the honeymoon period of full investment. Once I was fully committed to practicing empathy whenever possible, I began to conflate empathy with holding people accountable and establishing clear roles and goals. Through Dr. Roberts's guidance and my own experiences, I came to understand that the practicing of one does not eliminate the need for the other. Both are needed, and they work best when practiced in tandem.

Let me share with you one leader's journey through the stages of evolving empathy. Pay attention to the stages and behaviors that resonate with you, with an employee you are coaching, or with one of your leaders. Building awareness is key to developing your empathy muscle.

CASE STUDY: A PATH OF PATIENCE FROM CURIOUS TO REVOLUTIONARY

When I met DB, he led without an ounce of empathy. He was sought after as a turnaround leader at an automotive plant in South Carolina. He had succeeded at his mission—he produced the desired outcomes, but not without leaving dead bodies in the wake. He was excited during our first coaching session because he had heard about my former leadership approach and saw me as reinforcement for his take-no-prisoners approach. I knew there was a lot of transformative work that needed to happen with DB, and I knew it wouldn't happen overnight. Here's how he moved through the stages.

Curiosity

The manufacturing plants were in danger of losing contract renewals. Turnover was high. Leadership was lackluster. The union was threatening a strike, and the senior leadership was "soft." In the curiosity phase, DB did not disappoint. He asked all the questions you would expect at this phase.

- What about the union? Doesn't it seem as if they want the company to go under with their financially ridiculous demands?

- Some of these people are felons; shouldn't they be happy to have a job?

- We "make it or break it" in millions of dollars per minute. What do we do if people are not here and the lines shut down?

In the curiosity phase, it is common for people to be defensive. They present all the evidence they have in defense of the unempathetic status quo. They often believe that there must be a better way than "allowing" people to get away with abusing the system. In this phase, people struggle to acknowledge the inherent worth in people. In this case, the union stewards, the line workers, the senior leaders all were "less than" to DB.

Give It a Try #1: Consider a challenge you are struggling with and eager to resolve quickly. Put yourself in the curiosity stage. What questions do you ask? Write them down. Are your questions based in empathy for those involved in the solution (DB needs reliable long-term line people to help solve part of his problem), or are they based in indifference?

Resistance and Reluctance

The first day I walked into a training seminar with the frontline leaders, DB warned me that these people were "rough around the edges," so I might want to "dumb down" my language. For clarity, I always adjust the language I use to match the language of the people I'm with. However, it is not dumbing down. It is communicating effectively. When I am in the south, I use *ma'am* and *sir*, just like everyone else. When I instruct a group of academics, I share seminal source references. When facilitating a group of faith leaders, I try not to swear.

The session was focused on each leader understanding their leadership style and the strengths and liabilities associated with their leadership preferences. As usual, there were a couple of naturally empathetic leaders in the room, and they would share examples of how working on the line improved their relationships with the employees. They also shared examples of how they would seek out opportunities to work with the union to interpret the limits of the contract in ways that benefited the people. It was hard to refute the success of these stories.

DB landed in the resistance/reluctance zone. He was tired of fighting. He understood that the company's values stated that people were first, and he could not argue that point. He reluctantly believed that empathy was "fine" but resisted the idea that he could employ empathy *and* achieve his desired outcomes. Here's what his resistance and reluctance looked like:

- He took a sideline position of "I will not get in the way of these empathetic efforts, but I'll be here to pick up the pieces when they fail."

- He stopped defending unempathetic positions even though he still did not lead with empathy himself.

- He gave the leaders who had an empathetic orientation the leeway to try some things out.

Give It a Try #2: Identify one or two empathetic people in your organization, work group, community group—your circle of concern. Think of a time when they made a suggestion that was based in empathy. Did you consider it a viable option, or were you reluctant and resistant? Why?

Cautious Investment

One of the first empathetic approaches we tried was results-only work or self-directed work teams. The teams were all provided the same finance, quality, and safety information as the leaders. They were then asked to create their own charter. Many of the rules of the charter remained the same, with one major exception: people could share their vacation days if they wanted. (If someone needed time off but had none left on the books, a coworker could let them draw on their vacation time.) Incorporating this change was full of risk, but guess what? It worked. Now that they were better informed and were empowered to incorporate some changes, the line workers' sense of accountability for their work increased.

DB said, "Maybe you're onto something." Making things work excited DB, and now he had experienced his own successful outcome because of his decision to allow others to lead empathetically. In this cautious-investment phase, people, while they've experienced some success, are still vulnerable to slipping back into old ways, and DB was no exception. At the sign of any slippage in production or any new production problem, or whenever there would be "too much" people drama, DB would revert to his unempathetic leadership style.

Give It a Try #3: Think of a time in which you observed or participated in a people-over-policy scenario in which outcomes were achieved. If you haven't experienced a people-over-policy scenario (I'm really sorry), imagine the success of the empathetic suggestion from Give It a Try #2. Would/Did this motivate you to initiate a review of other policies and ways to put people first? Why or why not?

Full Investment

Today DB works for a different company. It has a company culture that is full of naturally empathetic people, so DB is still a bit like a fish out of water. It doesn't come naturally to him, but he continues to intentionally work on it, and he finds it strange when people don't want to lead with empathy. While he doesn't get it right 100 percent of the time, no one does. DB has not only fully embraced the practice of leading with empathy, but he has also progressed to inviting others to join the empathy revolution. When you reach full investment, you eagerly pass it on.

Give It a Try #4: Start getting comfortable talking about empathy. Initiate a conversation about empathy in your workplace with one person. Ask them what empathy means to them, and then share your perspective on empathy. Talk about how you both think it may or may not fit into your organization. Remember: Listen for understanding, not for judgment, validation, or accuracy, even if you disagree!

The Watch-Outs

DB wasn't exempt from stumbling along the way. Once he became fully invested in leading empathetically, he started to conflate being empathetic with many of the myths that cause people to balk at empathy in the first place. He began lowering his expectations. In another assignment at the senior leader level, he noticed that the team had major skill gaps. Instead of expecting that those gaps close, he thought being empathetic meant working around the gaps. He struggled for almost a year with this misconception. He became disheartened because he wasn't getting the turnaround results that he was used to. When he finally mentioned the scenario to me in a coaching session, we were able to get back on track. Establishing goal and role clarity for everyone on your team is not in contrast with empathy. Neither is setting clear objectives for which people must be held accountable.

This full process took DB approximately three years to navigate. The range is often three to five years, and while DB was a quick learner, he was also a patient one. Have patience with yourself as you move through this process. Don't buy into the microwave approach that insists people should change overnight, that as soon as we know better, we should do better. Changing our orientation to life and leading takes time, commitment, and patience.

When you review this scenario, what stage do you see yourself in right now? What stage do you want to be in? How will you get there? Changing our orientation to life and leading also takes focus and planning. Plan your next step!

STRETCHING YOUR MUSCLE

We've talked about the importance of awareness. Awareness of what empathy means to you and why. Awareness of opportunities throughout your day to practice empathy and what that feels like. Most of this awareness has centered within your own bubble, and that's a great starting point, but to really stretch your empathy muscle, it's time to develop your awareness of perspectives and experiences beyond your bubble.

One of the easiest ways to do that is to read fiction. Through fiction, we can experience the world as another gender, ethnicity, culture, sexuality, profession, or age and even experience another time period. Recent brain research suggests that reading literary fiction helps people develop empathy and critical thinking.

Check out some documentaries that explore different cultures. Attend a religious service outside your own. Intentionally engage in dialogue with someone who does not share your views on a subject. It can be politics, religion, education, parenting, etc. … the key is to practice listening for understanding and checking your judgment at the door.

Spend time in unfamiliar environments. Never been to traffic court? Have a seat there for an hour or two, and try to understand the experience from the view of the defendant, the plaintiff, the judge, the defense attorney, the prosecuting attorney, the arresting officer, the witnesses. In your observation, do people prevail over policy, or do policies prevail over people?

I've never been to traffic court, and my record appears to have zero moving violations. Not because I've never gotten a traffic ticket but because I can afford to hire an attorney to go for me. But my friend and colleague attorney David Bell provided me insight on the process.

> *We want people to obey the traffic laws, but how should that happen, and how should that be applied across society? In our courtroom locally, if somebody can't afford an attorney, they must come to court. And when they come to court, they often must sit for an hour or two waiting for their case to be called. But before that happens, they've had to take time off work or find childcare; they've had to take the time to get to court and pay for parking.*
>
> *When the time comes for them to stand up and represent themselves, they are on their own. Neither the judge nor the prosecutor is allowed to give them advice. As a result of their lack of resources, they may or may not resolve their case that day. If they don't resolve it, they must come back and repeat the process again. When the process for getting people to obey the traffic laws involves removing them from their family, from their job, for four to eight hours, it comes at a significant cost. That cost is borne primarily by individuals who don't have the money to opt out of the system by hiring a lawyer.*

Take some time to reflect on this very real scenario. How would you begin to look at changes to this process through the lens of empathy for the defendant while also considering the need for societal laws? I know that this is a massive issue to be solved, but I challenge you to come up with three ideas, baby steps, that might begin to shift awareness from policy over people to people over policy. What about the people who don't have the money to handle their parking and/or speeding tickets? Do you know what happens? Some people end up being incarcerated because of these types of issues. Now consider what that means when you have policies that exclude people with arrest records from your hiring pool.

WHEN ALL ELSE FAILS, OFFER GRACE

We are often expected to push through the pain and challenges that life throws at us and move forward with confidence. This is especially true if we are leaders or famous people. However, leaders and famous people are still people. When they fail us or don't live up to our expectations, we should offer them grace and kindness instead of judging or separating ourselves from them.

I was most guilty of separating myself from others, even if I didn't openly express it. Before my mother passed away, I recall avoiding people who spoke about their dead loved ones years after their passing. What I came to realize when my mom died was that grief is not linear. There were days when I would be perfectly fine. Then, my son graduated from high school, and my mom wasn't there. The sadness returned, and this was years later. Finally, I understood viscerally what I could not understand mentally.

> What may seem irrational to you is perfectly rational to someone else.

What may seem irrational to you is perfectly rational to someone else. They aren't necessarily irrational. It's simply how they experience the world. Don't punish others for not experiencing the world in the same way you do. I did not need to avoid people who were grieving. While it was not my experience at the time, I could have still practiced empathy. Granting people grace does not require experience; it only takes practice.

Chapter 7

Leading with Empathy Makes You Stronger

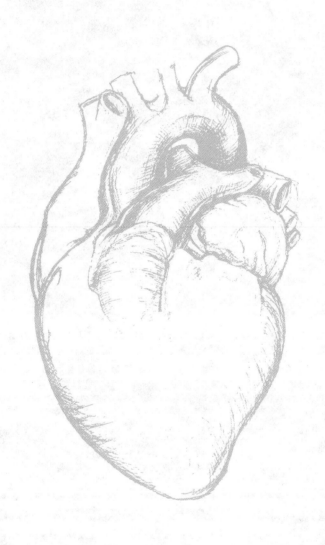

If only I'd known being nice to customers was so good for business, I'd have done it much earlier!

—MICHAEL O'LEARY, RYANAIR CEO

While O'Leary oversimplifies simply being "nice" as the solution to Ryanair's incredibly poor customer satisfaction record, he had to make a 180-degree turn from his previous anticustomer approach. He used to charge customers who forgot their boarding pass sixty euros for "being so stupid" saying things like, "You're not getting a refund so **** off. We don't want to hear your sob stories. What part of 'no refund' don't you understand?"[19] ...

Later he acknowledged that in order to implement plans to grow from 80 million to over 110 million in 5 years, he had to actively listen and respond to customers.[20] This required him to recognize and understand what a satisfied experience looks like for his customers and then take action on that understanding. It is critical to a company's overall success. Yes, he was meeting his numbers and the company was highly profitable, but his brutal cost-cutting methods at the expense of his customers' satisfaction was limiting Ryanair's growth.

---

19   Skift, "The Most Wonderfully Offensive Quotes From Ryanair Boss Michael O'Leary," skift.com, September 5, 2012, https://skift.com/2012/09/05/ryanair-boss-michael-oleary-gives-best-quotes-in-the-industry/.

20   Conor Humphries, "Ryanair unveils new strategy: 'be nice to customers,'" reuters.com, September 20, 2013, https://www.reuters.com/article/us-ryanair/ryanair-unveils-new-strategy-be-nice-to-customers-idUSBRE98J0DF20130920.

In 2014, when board members shared that they had observed people crying at boarding gates, that their own family members refused to fly Ryanair, and that they were often verbally attacked at dinner parties over Ryanair's awful customer service, O'Leary was forced to concede that what their customers thought and wanted did matter and that it was time for him to listen.[21]

This newfound perspective doesn't mean that O'Leary suddenly believes in caring about people, and that's okay. Leading with empathy isn't about spreading the love; it's about listening for understanding and strategically acting on that understanding. In changing this approach with his customers, O'Leary will also be changing the experience for his employees. No longer will they feel compelled to berate customers and enforce fines for minor infractions. O'Leary has conceded that policy cannot always rule and that enforcing rules that "piss people off for no good reason" isn't good business. Employees now have the authority to waive fees when a customer's luggage has a minor weight overage. The ripple effect will slowly build momentum.

As a result, Ryanair's customer-satisfaction rating the moment they step off the plane has reached 81 percent—vastly different from being known as the airline with the least-satisfied customers. Ryanair's bottom line? It saw a net profit increase of $123 million between 2015 and 2016.

So, how do you begin to reorient your company culture to one that is based in empathy? I've provided five empathetic leadership strategies below to get you started.

---

21   Tyler Falk, "Ryanair really is getting more customer friendly: Believe it or not, Ryanair is trying to make its customers happy," zdnet.com, October 27, 2013, https://www.zdnet.com/article/ryanair-really-is-getting-more-customer-friendly/.

EMPATHETIC LEADERSHIP STRATEGIES

1. Vision Focus

2. Get Curious and Engage

3. Coaching and Development

4. Listen Empathetically

5. Power of Seven Second Chances

STRATEGY ONE: VISION FOCUS

I'm not going to go into detail on how and why to develop a vision that can be clearly communicated; there are hundreds of other books out there that will do that. What I want to share is how to create a vision that will lead your company toward an empathetic culture.

A key component of any vision is communicating clearly why you are asking people to follow you. Think about that. Leaders seek understanding of their why, and they do this because they know that if people don't "get it," as in don't empathize with the why of their vision, it's going to be far more difficult to gain the level of com-

> A key component of any vision is communicating clearly why you are asking people to follow you.

mitment required. How much more committed do you think those you are leading would be if they felt that their needs, their whys, were also better understood?

- Employees who feel heard are 4.6 times more likely to feel empowered to perform to the best of their abilities.

- Employees who feel heard increase their engagement with the company, and increased engagement results in

  □ greater profitability—23 percent

  □ eighty-one percent less absenteeism

  □ significant decrease in turnover[22]

It is my hope that, since you are still reading, you have bought into the benefits of empathy and its place in business. Now you're ready to communicate that belief with others, to establish a common mindset of building an empathetic culture.

Common mindset. The power of a mission and vision communication is providing everyone in the organization with a road map on how they are going to be part of something grand and exciting. Start with your leadership team. Talk to them honestly about the concept of empathy and how you see it fitting into the company culture. Invite them to provide honest feedback, and remember to listen for understanding when they do. Acknowledge what this change will require.

Change readiness. Most significant vision and mission statements represent a deviation from the past. They represent a rallying call for a departure from business as usual. They require that people are going to have to think and act differently. For that reason, underneath the excitement will be apprehension, anxiety, and fear of the unknown. Share with your leadership team that this is an opportunity

22

for you all to learn together and that mistakes will be made. Walk with them through strategies 3, 4, 5, and 6.

STRATEGY TWO: GET CURIOUS AND ENGAGE

The best way to find out what is going on, how people are interacting, and what's working and what isn't is to observe and engage. My number one go to is my gemba walk. This continuous-improvement practice of walking the floors of where the actual work is taking place to observe employees and processes is a great starting place. Once you have observed, you can determine the best way to engage.

Examples of intentional engagement include the following:

- **Undercover boss:** This is a terrific way to observe and engage alongside your employees. But remember, the purpose is to do the job of others so that you understand the challenges they face. It is *not* to secretly check up on your employees.

- **Onboarding:** Have leaders in new roles spend a "day in the life" of their direct reports and the internal clients upstream and downstream.

- **Service projects:** Do service projects with your team in the community where you work. This is a wonderful way to find out what your employees care about outside the office.

- **The amazing race in schools:** Go visit the homes of every student before the first month of the school year is over. This method might be adapted (e.g., visit every client site) for other types of agencies.

If you do not believe that the community you are engaging in is worthy, begin with a spirit of curiosity. Curiosity does not require that we believe that the community we are engaging with deserves dignity. However, it is important to understand that we run the risk of being disrespectful or offensive when a culture of dignity is absent.

Dignity versus Respect

By now you have realized that dignity and respect are resounding components of empathy, and while I have provided definitions and examples previously, here I want to clarify the differences between dignity and respect, things that are often confused, especially when positions of power and authority are at play.

Here are definitions adopted by the Cultures of Dignity organization:

- **Dignity:** From the Latin word *dignitas*, meaning "to be worthy."

  - As in: All people have the right to be recognized for their inherent humanity and treated ethically. Dignity is a given. You just have it, and no one can take it away.

- **Respect:** From the Latin word *respectus*, meaning "to look back at."

  - As in showing admiration for someone because of their abilities, qualities, or achievements. Respect is earned. You are respected by others for what you have achieved and experienced and how you have handled yourself as you have achieved accomplishments.[23]

When it comes to a relationship, we commonly frame being respectful as being polite and obedient and following the rules. In this context, questioning the rules or challenging the person enforcing the rules is often perceived as defiant, rude, and disrespectful and is subject to punishment.

The questions then become these:

- Should someone respect someone in a position of authority who abuses power?

- Should you respect someone who doesn't treat others with dignity?

- Even if they're older than you?

- Even if they have more seniority than you?

- Even if they have more experience than you?

- Even if they have more money or power than you?

- If dignity is a given that can't be taken away, what does it look like to treat someone you don't respect with dignity?

If we use dignity as our anchor and ground our work in the belief that every person has value, then we can separate people's abusive actions from their essential humanity. For example, there may be a boss at work who belittles, bullies, or embarrasses people under them in front of others. The boss does not need to be respected based on their behavior, but they need to be treated with dignity. It may look

---

23 Cultures of Dignity, "What Is Dignity?" culturesofdignity.com, January 23, 2020, https://culturesofdignity.com/what-is-dignity/.

like the same thing, treating the person with respect versus treating that person with dignity, but it is an important distinction. Respect acknowledges the behavior, while dignity teaches the importance of civility and humanity.

STRATEGY THREE: COACHING AND DEVELOPMENT

Empathy can be developed. I hope you have also bought into this idea by now. But what do you do if you aren't a people developer in general? What if you are so focused on results that you have no time for long-term development of people's empathy muscles? What happens when you think building empathy in others isn't your job or, worse, is risky to your own career? Make an intentional plan.

Empathetic leaders must be able to observe the realities of today while also focusing clearly ahead. When empathetic leaders possess strategic agility, they can anticipate future consequences and trends related to people development accurately. They understand that failing to provide targeted and differentiated professional development has consequences. This is especially true for executive-level leaders. An orientation toward the future at the most influential levels is necessary to sustain a business. No one would argue against that.

Consequently, the skills of the people must be considered far into the future as well. Therefore, if there are performance gaps (e.g., empathy gaps), we must begin working on them. Good leaders can articulately paint credible pictures and visions of possibilities and likelihoods rallying others around their vision—for the organization and for the people. The organization is simply a conglomeration of the people within it. Coaching and developing the people is a competitive and breakthrough strategy.

Many leaders think development is taking a training class. I once had no idea how development really happened for people. Skilled people developers provide challenging assignments specifically designed to build empathy. These leaders engage in development discussions often and are aware of each person's career goals. The development plans combine career goals with empathy and stretch people to accept developmental projects.

Here are some key areas I have found to be helpful in the coaching of empathy in others.

Prepare for Empathy Detractors and Resisters:

There will always be those who don't buy it, have seen it all before, haven't yet seen a mission or vision come true. They may be private about it or come at you in public. It's important to first identify anyone on your leadership team who fits this mindset and provide them additional coaching outside the group before you communicate the mission and vision to the company.

When the leadership team is in alignment, work with them to produce ten critical questions that might come up. "What happened to last year's brand-new mission that we've already abandoned? I don't think that will work. Why do we have to get all touchy-feely? Everything is working fine the way it is." Be prepared for the most likely criticisms. Mentally rehearse how, as a team, you might respond to questions. Determine when you are ready to present to everyone in the company.

When presented, listen patiently to people's concerns, protecting their feelings but also reinforcing the perspective of why the change is needed. Deconstruct negative positions, not the people. Show patience toward the unconverted; maintain a light touch. Remember, there was a time during the crafting of this vision that you were not convinced. Invite alternative suggestions to reach the same outcome. In the end, thank everyone for their time and input, and reaffirm that the company will be moving in this direction. You may, on occasion, need to pull a specific person aside and say, "I understand all your worries and have tried to respond to them, but the train is moving on. If there are other ways I can help you in this process, let me know. I also encourage you to consider whether this is still the right fit for you moving forward."

> **Invest Time:** I know that finding time is often the biggest challenge that leaders face. I have asked thousands of leaders what gets in the way of them being the best leaders they could be. Their answer? Time! They just don't have the time to be great leaders and coaches. Korn Ferry states that "you need to allocate about 8 hours per year per direct report. If you have seven direct reports, that's 7 of 220 working days or 3 percent of your time."[24]

This feels low to me. The coaching and development parts of my role take up most of my time. However, it's not additive time. When we are working to develop empathy in ourselves and others, the work is done in tandem (on the job) with the other aspects of our work. It is not separate and apart from our tasks. On-the-job training is a practical approach to acquiring new competencies and skills needed for a job in a real, or close to real, working environment.

People commonly think of on-the-job training as the use of tools or equipment in a live-work practice, simulated, or training environment. That's too narrow. Everyone can develop empathy

---

24   Robert Eichinger and Michael Lombardo, FYI For Your Improvement: A guide For Development and Coaching, (Lominger Ltd Inc, 2006).

while working. Remember, meaningful development is not in the stress-reduction business. It is not cozy or safe; it comes from varied, stressful, even adverse tasks that require we learn to do something new or different or fail. Real development involves real work that the person isn't experienced with. Your patience and support will be necessary during this time. Making mistakes is part of life, and it happens with or without empathy. Be careful not to make causal relationships between mistakes and building empathy muscles.

Find the Empathetic Patterns and Build upon Them: Help those you are coaching look for patterns in the situations and problems they deal with. What succeeded and what failed? What was common to each success, or what was present in each failure but never present in a success? Focus on the successes; failures are easier to analyze but don't in themselves tell you what would work. Comparing successes yields more information. The goal is to help them reduce insights to principles or rules of thumb that might be repeatable. Ask them what they have learned to increase their skills and understanding that would make them more empathetic managers or professionals. Ask them what they can do now that they couldn't do a year ago. Reinforce this and encourage more of it. Developing is learning in as many ways as possible.

Sell Long-Term Empathy Development. Part of developing others is convincing people that tough, new, challenging, and different assignments are good for them. In follow-up studies of successful executives, more than 90 percent reported that a boss in their past nearly forced them to take a scary job assignment that they wanted to turn down. That assignment turned out to be the most developmental for them.[25] Empathy is that way. However, empathy isn't developed quickly. It took me almost eight years to build my empathy muscle to the point that felt natural to me and at which other people were able to recognize it. Don't be alarmed by that timeline. I told you I might be the worst person to tell you about empathy. In my professional practice, the timeline is much shorter. The average person can develop empathy within three to five years. Before you balk at that range, consider the average tenure of the leaders in your organization. If it is greater than three years, you have the time.

Because this type of transformative behavior takes time, although you may have a sense of urgency for someone's transformation, it's important not to share your timeline with others. Setting a timeline in which to demonstrate transformation can create undue pressure and push an individual to feign empathy to get you to move on. The process will have enough opportunities for people to fight the urge to revert to a prior way of thinking; pressuring someone to expedite the process will make that fight more difficult.

This is long-term development, one that requires getting out of our comfort zone on a regular basis. A leader's job is to help convince people on the way up to get out of their comfort zone and accept opportunities to build their empathy muscle even if they may not initially see it as useful or leading anywhere.

Build Perspective: Help those you lead expand their perspectives. Give the people under your leadership who have

---

25   Robert W. Eichinger and Michael M. Lombardo, FYI: For Your Improvement, (Lominger Ltd., 2006).

the potential for increased responsibilities and challenges assignments that take them outside their typical functions, unit, or business. Volunteer them for cross-boundary task forces. Have them attend meetings that include people from other areas. Open the world for them so that they can better judge for themselves what's out there and what part of it they want. Ask empathy questions when making decisions, and encourage others to do the same.

In addition to these questions

- What are the pros and cons?

- What are the logical consequences? But what about ... ?

- What's wrong with this?

- Why aren't we following through now?

ask these questions:

- What do we like and dislike?

- What impact will this have on people?

- How can we make everyone happy?

- What's beneficial in this?

- What about the people who will be hurt?

- How will people feel about this?[26]

---

26   Naomi L. Quenk and Jean M. Kummerow, MBTI Step II Profile – Form Q (R), themyersbriggs.com, accessed: October 13, 2022, https://shop.themyersbriggs.com/en/mbtiproducts.aspx?pc=49.

The Three Cs: Confidence, Commitment, Celebration

When I came to appreciate that people demonstrating empathy toward me helped me become a better (in every sense of the word) person, there were three things I had to always keep at the forefront of my mind to stay focused on leading with empathy. I find these particularly valuable when I am coaching around empathy, and I want to share them with you.

1. **Confidence:** While I am still not always fully competent in demonstrating empathy, I have the belief that a world with empathy is better than a world without—no exception. I lean in to the times when someone has been empathetic to me and what the result was. Through that lens, I usually gain renewed confidence that I can continue to build my empathy muscle.

2. **Commitment:** Every day, without exception, someone will present a situation that they believe should be void of empathy. I am committed to the idea that understanding cognitively, feeling what other people feel (even hate; I hate meanness and therefore understand hating and can better respond to it), being motivated to help someone besides myself, and responding appropriately are necessary characteristics of a healthy, strong society.

3. **Celebration:** When practicing empathy works out, I keep track. I look for empathy and find joy in those moments. I need celebrations to give me more strength and resolve about taking an empathetic stance in the face of logic and reason at times, especially considering that logical, reasonable objectivity is my natural inclination.

Watch-Outs: There are a few obstacles to watch out for while helping others build empathy.

- Working on the empathy development of a few people at the expense of many people

- Being overly optimistic about how much people can grow

- Not believing people can really develop empathy

- Not modeling or providing the confidence, commitment, and celebrations essential to helping others develop empathy.

STRATEGY FOUR: LISTEN EMPATHETICALLY

Many people struggle to listen. When we try to listen, we are often distracted thinking about our own responses. If the person speaking hesitates, we cut them off and finish their sentences, often interrupting so we can offer solutions even when we don't fully understand the problem (or whether there even is one!). We also prioritize our level of listening depending on who the speaker is. While we listen to some people intently, there are others we listen to with disinterest, and then there are those we simply tune out altogether. Not listening attentively limits our ability to learn about and from those we interact with, reducing our ability to be empathetic.

The key is to pay attention to how you listen. Spend a day paying attention to who you listen to and how you listen to them. Make a list of the people you listened to (whether you had to or not). Now categorize how you listened to each of those individuals. Mark *I* for intently, *D* for disinterest, and *T* for those you tuned out. If you have *D*s and *T*s, practice changing those to *I*s. Once a week do this type of check-in to see how you are improving and whether there are patterns in how you listen. For example, are you able to listen intently to people you disagree with, or do they always show up as a *D* or a *T* on your list?

Encourage your leadership team to participate in this same exercise. Ask your team for feedback on how they feel you listen—and remember to listen to their feedback for understanding and not what you think is accurate!

Here are some tips for practicing attentive listening:

- Keep your mouth closed and eyes on the speaker. Contrary to widely held belief, don't engage in head nods, uh-huhs, or other physical gestures that simply make you *appear* to be listening.

- Have the patience to hear people out.

- Accurately restate the opinions of others even when you disagree.

In our leadership training sessions through Lively Paradox, we engage in a couple of exercises that increase our capacity to listen in ways that enhance our understanding and build our empathy muscles. In our first exercise, we have people pair up and take turns speaking and listening about an experience in their life that was challenging. The speaker talks for two minutes while the other person in the pair listens empathetically. They do not listen to respond, only to understand.

Once the first person has finished sharing, we invite the participants to swap roles: the speaker is now listener, and listener is now speaker. During the debrief, some amazing things happen. Speakers will often share that it felt good to be able to talk about a time when they were challenged without someone interjecting. It's also common for listeners to share that they found it refreshing to be able to just listen and understand with no other expectations.

A second exercise we engage our participants in is listening to or watching a station that they typically don't. As an example, if you tend to watch a more liberal-leaning political news station, we ask you to listen to a conservative one. If you tend to focus on local news, we ask you to listen to global news. If you tend to get your news from more neutral sources, we ask for you to find one that is overtly leaning to one side or another on a topic. Then we set the timer. For two minutes each participant is asked to listen to or watch the news through the supportive mindset focused on listening for understanding only. We remind the participants that regardless of what the other person is saying or doing, they are to keep in mind that what the speaker says makes total sense to the speaker. We are so programmed to listen for judgment that this exercise is truly enlightening for our participants.

We recognize that this practice of empathetic listening doesn't come naturally to everyone. There are differences in lived experiences and other factors that must be considered. Regardless of those differences, when there is a personal desire to engage in empathetic listening, lives inevitably change. People become more attuned to their own proclivity to speak more and listen less. They then flip the script and do just the opposite; they listen more and speak less, with the listening focused on understanding the experience and not the accuracy of the content. Another result of this practice is a willingness to truly understand issues from the perspective of others, even when they have opposing viewpoints.

> When there is a personal desire to engage in empathetic listening, lives inevitably change.

I encourage you to engage your leadership team in these empathy-building exercises. Data indicates that you will reap the rewards.

- Effective listening correlates positively with staff productivity.

- Listening well reduces absenteeism, aids employee retention, improves cross-functional team communication, and results in more informed senior leadership.

- According to the US Bureau of Labor Statistics, forty-seven million people (about twice the population of New York) quit their jobs between 2020 and 2022 in part because leaders were not listening and adjusting to their needs.

- Employees disengage from conversations when they feel like their leaders are not listening. This results in problems growing out of control by the time leadership is aware of them.[27]

STRATEGY FIVE: THE POWER OF SEVEN SECOND CHANCES

What would you want to see happen or have done if you were sitting on the other side of the boardroom table? How well did you perform your first year of teaching, of leading? Choose a role you were hired

---

27 Psychology Compass, "4 ways to reduce absenteeism by tackling employee disengagement," https://psychologycompass.com/blog/absenteeism/.

Bernard T. Ferrari, "The executive's guide to better listening," McKinsey Quarterly, February 1, 2012, https://www.mckinsey.com/featured-insights/leadership/the-executives-guide-to-better-listening.

Hypercontext, "5 Tips for better cross-functional collaboration," hypercontext.com, November 16, 2021, https://hypercontext.com/blog/communication/tips-for-better-cross-functional-collaboration#:~:text=Another%20important%20factor%20in%20effective,what%20they%20don't%20understand.

to do and think about the mistakes you made that first year. What action was taken when you screwed up? Were you given another chance or two? Those are the types of questions Dr. Roberts wants us all to consider when we rush to judge and decide to fire, expel, or take any action that will adversely affect the individual who made a mistake, who broke policy. Dr. Roberts believes everyone deserves seven chances and maybe even fourteen! Here's how that concept developed.

Several years ago, the deans responsible for student discipline approached Dr. Roberts with concern about a student who had just come to enroll at the school. They expressed their sincere concern about the appropriateness of enrolling this particular student, who had tattoos all over his face and neck, had been kicked out of every other school, and was known to be a gang leader.

Dean: "Dr. Roberts, we cannot enroll this student. He would be disruptive to the school and could tear down what we have worked so hard to build."

Dr. Roberts: "If we don't accept him, where will he go to school? We have an obligation to give him at least one chance to get it right, don't we?"

Dean: "Okay, we give him a chance, and the first time he breaks policy, we can expel him."

Dr. Roberts: "No."

Dean: "Then what?"

Dr. Roberts: "We give him one more chance."

Dean: "So after that, then we can expel him, because, Doc, I know that before the week is over, he's going to definitely commit at least two infractions."

Dr. Roberts: "Then I want you to give him a chance for each day of the week, because if he's going to violate our policies at least once a day, give him at least one week to get it right."

The dean persisted: "Okay, so after seven chances, we can expel him."

Dr. Roberts: "Multiply seven times two, and then you can expel him."

When I walked away in my moment of reflection, I thought to myself, I don't know too many people who have been given fourteen chances to get something right and didn't manage to get it right. And that conversation was the birth of my public commitment to make sure every student at our school receives at least seven second chances.

Prior to this verbalization of his seven second chances, Dr. Roberts had come to the concept of multiple chances based on a pivotal experience with one of his students.

I had to realize that when parents drop their child off or put them on the bus, they're sending us their absolute best child. They don't keep the good ones at home and send us the bad ones. And it is incumbent upon me and every other adult in our schools to understand two things. What are parents expecting of us, and what are our students thinking and expecting of us?

This thought process requires us to, every single day, put ourselves in the proverbial shoes and uniform of each child who knocks on our doors. Those experiences of putting myself in the student's shoes impact how I make decisions around whether to keep a student in school or suspend them, whether a student should receive an F versus a D. Those are decisions that significantly impact a student's life. A pivotal lesson for me when I was growing into my own empathetic leadership orientation was when I allowed myself to prioritize policies and protocols over people. I suspended one particular student repeatedly, despite his potential, and eventually he dropped out of school. I had never put myself in that student's shoes. I had not empathetically considered the lifelong impact that the stringent enforcement of policy would have on this student. That student is now serving a multiple life sentence in prison.

That was a life-changing experience that led Dr. Roberts to be ferocious and uncompromising in his journey as an empathetic person and an empathetic leader. Today he knows that suspensions are the greatest cause for a student ending up incarcerated.

I can never allow myself to backslide, and so every day there's a lot of intentionality on my part to try to remain in this space. There are times when I'm challenged, and that's when I return to questions like, What was I like as a first-year teacher? What happened that time when I accidentally, without putting on my signal, cut someone off at a stoplight, and now someone is doing it to me? What happens when someone must show up late to a meeting? What happens when I must decide whether to give someone a second opportunity to meet an assignment?

And what I've learned is that, contrary to the belief of some, my commitment to engaging with empathy hasn't made me weaker as a leader. It hasn't compromised the bottom line in ways that

negatively impact people's lives. The downside to leading relent-
lessly from an empathetic orientation is the delayed achievement
of goals. My team and I always meet our goals, but we don't
always achieve them within the timeline that someone or a body
of people in a position of power said that we should achieve them
in. But I've decided I can live with that, because in the wake
of achieving those goals with a little bit of delay, we improved
people's lives.

When Dr. Roberts first introduced me to his concept of seven second chances, I was more than skeptical. I mean, is no one held accountable for their actions? While I have come to a better appreciation and understanding of multiple chances and I have incorporated it into my empathetic leadership practice, I must be honest and say that I still struggle with it. I sometimes struggle with what feels like the incongruence of chances and accountability—where should the line be drawn? I cannot always make it to fourteen chances, and I'm okay with that. I believe we all need to find our balance. That's a bit easier if we are clear about our nonnegotiables.

NONNEGOTIABLES

There are circumstances that Dr. Roberts has shared with me that I believe go to the extremes. But in those moments, I can still listen for understanding, I can still learn from his empathetic experience, and I can still determine what balance means for me. It's not unusual for people to jump to extreme circumstances about why a new concept they have been introduced to won't work. It happens in my workshops all the time. Inevitably, someone in the room will say, "Well, what about … ?" Then that person will go on to talk about the most egregious situations they can imagine. I understand this thinking.

Whenever I get exposed to something I am a little resistant to, I, too, start to think of all the ways in which it simply will not work. After all, I once thought no one was deserving of even one chance: the idea of seven chances was beyond ridiculous. While I want you to think about all the ways in which you *can*, there are times—some nonnegotiables—when we just cannot lean in to empathy in the way that others might.

Establish your nonnegotiables. For me, there are two nonnegotiables—value misalignment and legal, moral, and ethical violations.

Value Misalignment

Occasionally, someone will join my team who absolutely is not aligned with the values of the organization. We hired someone into the organization specifically to help us create some standard operating procedures, identify some frequently asked questions, and develop timelines for clients to follow. He believed that the world should be very scheduled. "Plan your work and work your plan" was his motto. I am an engineer. I can relate. I value a good process. However, one of the three values at Lively Paradox is flexibility—this is a value we make clear to everyone. We understand and know the clients will come to us with a variety of different situations. Because our mission is to create a more equitable, inclusive, and just world, I personally demand that I am in alignment with this vision. To do so requires flexibility. Our clients come from a range of diverse backgrounds and industries. It is a requirement of everyone who joins our team to be flexible in order to meet the client's needs.

Standard is the antithesis to diversity. Having rigid timelines and rules will limit the opportunities. In short, we value being flexible, being inclusive, and allowing organizations to identify where they can plug into the work. Our new employee was out of alignment with this value. When he did not get his timelines met, he would pout. When I would demonstrate flexibility to support a client, changing dates and other meetings on the schedule, he would completely shut down. When I called him to discuss it, he would smile and grin and then offer some backhanded comments about how the organization was a "mess." If he couldn't find a standard operating procedure, he would get irritated. Never mind that he had been hired to create those procedures. One day he classified my relentless insistence on flexibility and my desire to have him lean in to his role as the organizer as a toxic work environment.

I fired him.

Now, some people would say, "Nicole, what about your power of seven second chances?" Others might say, "Are you kidding me? You're the empathy lady." Hear me out. I understood very clearly that if I thought what this employee thought, I would do what he did. I listened intently to him. I felt the emotions he felt. In fact, I am intimately aware of what it feels like to work in a toxic environment. I imagined what that would be like for me, and it made my stomach hurt. That day, I fired him for me, for the organization, and for him. When an organization has a mission, the employees will be happy only when they are in alignment with that mission. When the employees are out of alignment, it makes for an extremely uncomfortable experience for them, and it could create a toxic environment for everyone else.

To be clear, this is not about cultural fit. In fact, I hate that term. This is about value alignment. Lively Paradox's value of flexibility means a lot to me and my team. Our new employee's values of sticking to a plan more than anything else was important to him. We have a right to our values, and he has a right to his, and it was clear they were never going to align, and that is okay; it just means we can't work together. If he understood and was aligned with the mission, vision, and values of the organization and he grounded his decisions in those values every day, he would've had an extensive career with Lively Paradox.

In the same way that employees must adhere to the values of the organization, so, too, must its leaders. I am a religious person. I pray a lot. My faith values are an important part of who I am. They are my personal values, and the truth is they don't completely align with Lively Paradox's value of inclusive leadership. I cannot assert my personal values on those I work with if they don't align with the company values: I cannot come in and pray over everyone all day. If I did, I would be misaligned with the company's value of inclusive leadership. It would be exclusionary to people who are not religious.

When challenges arise, look to your values for clarification. A boss who meets his numbers every month but also berates employees isn't in alignment with a company whose value is respect for others. This doesn't mean that the person should be immediately fired; it means that you need to address the misalignment, and that includes taking the time to understand why there is misalignment and providing chances for them to get on board. How many chances? That needs to be determined by you. Dr. Roberts would suggest enough chances so that when you do make the decision to terminate, you won't have any doubts about whether it was the right decision or not.

Empathy and Our Legal, Moral, and Ethical Parameters

When Jonathan Ross ran a stoplight and rammed into my mother's car in a stolen vehicle while drunk and high on drugs, he had clearly broken several laws—eight, to be exact. He had violated legal, moral, and ethical parameters. So, I feel prepared when people ask me, "Nicole, how can we practice empathy when someone makes a decision that isn't legally, ethically, and morally sound?

I feel even more prepared when they ask me, "What if my moral and ethical values are different?" Morally, I have no alignment with Mr. Ross. I also did not agree with his choices that day. However, I have a good understanding of the challenges he faced that led him to those decisions that fateful day. I also can connect emotionally with the incredible pain he must have felt in order to make the series of choices that landed him in prison for fifteen years. I believe he was mortified and inconsolable once he learned about the impact of his choices on countless people's lives. And while not every law is morally and ethically sound, the ones he violated were. It is not lost on me that if he had access to wealth, he might not have received the sentence he received. However, following the law is a nonnegotiable for most of us, even when we disagree with its existence.

Inside most organizations we are not faced with egregious events like this daily. It is more likely that we must deal with issues of sexual harassment, theft, tardiness, or committing multiple infractions of varying degrees. Making a commitment to lead from a place of empathy in these instances still should not be taken lightly. They are still legally, ethically, or morally wrong. Following the associated policies and rules should be nonnegotiable. Leading with empathy should be a nonnegotiable as well. Firing someone is one of the weightiest decisions a leader can make. Dr. Roberts has some insight on how to balance empathy with solid legal, ethical, and moral decision-making.

> When a leader has made a termination decision, I always ask how they spent their next twenty-four or forty-eight hours after making that decision. Most of them will say that they spent a lot of time reflecting and second-guessing whether they made the right decision, because they know it impacted and changed

the person's life. Where I sit now as a leader—and this sounds contradictory to being an empathetic leader—whenever I decide to remove or terminate, I go home and sleep very well. And the difference is I would've given that person an exhaustive number of opportunities to get it right. See, accountability doesn't have to occur within a measure of strong accountability, nor must it occur within a specific timeline. Unless an immediate decision must be made based on a morally, ethically, or legally egregious act, accountability should be married to support and coaching. My chances are offered until I get to the point where I can say to the person sitting across the table from me, "Look, you've done good work here, but after exhausting all our attempts to support you, this is no longer the right place for you to be," and then go home with no doubt that the right decision was made.

Conclusion

Join the Empathy Revolution

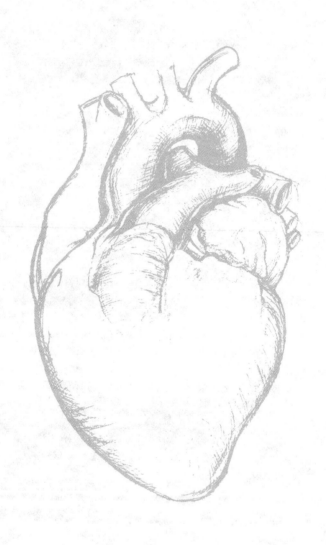

*We need empathy to create a new kind of
revolution. Not an old-fashioned revolution
built on new laws, institutions, or policies, but a
radical revolution in human relationships.*

—ROMAN KRZNARIC

I'm going to be honest with you right up to the end. I am not experienced at, nor do I feel confident about, organizing people to address a common cause that I alone cannot control. So again, I say that I might be the worst person to tell you about empathy, and I'll add, I might be even worse at leading an empathy revolution.

But here I am, choosing to lead the charge.

Why? Because I am committed to living and leading with empathy, and that requires me to keep getting out of my comfort zone and pushing myself to do what does not feel natural. Empathy is a lifelong practice. A practice that I believe will benefit us all.

I need your help.

Let's break down what that looks like.

First you must trust in the purpose and power of empathy. Remember when I encouraged you to identify what sparked your empathy? If you haven't done that yet, I encourage you to do it now. To get started, reflect on the following:

- In the context of what you now understand empathy to be, think about the first time you experienced empathy, either giving or receiving.

- What did that feel like, and why do you think it made you feel that way?

- What has been your most powerful experience with empathy? What about your most powerful nonempathetic experience?

- Think of two people in your life, one you see as empathetic and one who is not. How does your relationships with these individuals differ because of their level or lack of empathy?

- Right now, today, how does empathy make your feel, what do you see as its benefits and/or negative effects, and what form does it take in your life? Write your thoughts down.

Once you understand what sparked your empathy, you are ready to engage in a disciplined approach to your empathy practice. I'm not asking you to try to empathize with the world or even everyone in your neighborhood, office, or community. I'm asking you to start practicing empathy daily with the people in your circle of concern. Choose five of those people to get you started. Maybe one is your spouse, two are coworkers, and two are your children. Now discipline yourself to practicing empathy—both giving and receiving—with at least one of those people every day. This will be challenging at first. If you are as far off the empathy spectrum as I was when I first began my journey, it's going to require a lot of awareness and attention on your part to

> Once you understand what sparked your empathy, you are ready to engage in a disciplined approach to your empathy practice.

stick with the plan and to practice empathy daily. But you can do it, and I promise you will be a better person for it.

You'll have your relapses; you'll lose awareness from time to time. But as soon as you realize it, you need to jump back on the empathy train. Because, like anything else, the longer you let yourself slip, the harder it is to get back on track.

You've developed your trust in the purpose and power of empathy. You've disciplined yourself to a daily practice of empathy. Now, it's time to fully commit, and that requires accountability. Accountability will look different for everyone. Maybe every night you write down your empathetic experiences for that day and determine how you can do better tomorrow. Or you may want to hold yourself accountable by letting others know about your empathy practice and asking them for feedback on how your practice with them is going. Are they feeling understood by you?

For those who would like to be accountable to and celebrate empathy successes with others who are also intentionally practicing empathy, I have created an online platform to do just that.

As you become more confident and comfortable with your empathy practice, expand your reach. Intentionally practice empathy with people beyond your inner circle, nurture others to be empathetic, and watch its ripple effect.

Janice Toben, in her TED talk, shared a beautiful story of the transformative power of collective empathy, and I want to share it with you here.[28]

Before a woman of the Bembe tribe in South Africa is about to give birth, she gathers a bunch of her friends, and they go out into the wilderness together and meditate. In their

---

28 Janice Toben, "The Power of Collective Empathy," March 1, 2014, https://www.youtube.com/watch?v=aCfdSA3xcxw.

meditation they listen for a resonant sound, a song of the child who's about to come into the world. Once they have heard the child's song, they return to the village and sing that song to that child at their birth. They also sing that song at significant times in the individual's life, such as when they start school, when they graduate school, at moments related to marriage, and at their death.

Apart from those significant moments in one's life, the only other time they will sing the song is when the child has done something unkind or did something that was wrong. In those moments, the whole community gathers and encircles the person and tells the person about every good and beautiful thing they've ever done in their life, every strength they possess. They intentionally push their love and their empathy out to this person who's messed up, and they will do this for hours and sometimes days. At the end of that time, they have a ceremony and a party and sing the song again. Toben refers to this tradition as an example of the power of collecting empathy and gathering it in to remind us that we are always in this "how do I, who am I, what am I" process of our lives, and we are all a transformative force with the ability to create collective empathy.

Before you can truly lead with empathy, you must first understand and learn to practice empathy as an individual. Let this Fourteen Days of Empathy Practice be the start of your empathy journey. Make your first ripple, create collective empathy, and become a member of the empathy revolution!

Let's jump-start your journey now.

Getting Started

Week One:

Notice Empathy

DAY 1: HEALTH

Focus: When you are tired, hungry, chronically stressed, and with poor focus, it will be harder to enter the experience of another. The paradox is that empathy can help to keep you healthy.

Medical research estimates as much as **90 percent** of illness and disease is stress related. Emotional stress is a major contributing factor to the six leading causes of death in the United States: cancer, coronary heart disease, accidental injuries, respiratory disorders, cirrhosis of the liver, and suicide.[29]

Empathy can lower stress. Empathy promotes abilities that help us handle stress. Studies show that when we can regulate our emotions, we are better able to relate to others in positive ways.[30] This is known as **emotion regulation**, which is the ability to take in the experiences of others without being overwhelmed.

Although stress may be brought on by many different things, it is processed in our bodies in similar ways. Stress keeps us ready for action, but being on "ready, set" all the time is unhealthy. When we practice empathy, we can regulate ourselves emotionally. The

---

29 Clemson Extension, "Stress Management for the Health of It," nasdonline.org, November 1997, https://nasdonline.org/1445/d001245/stress-management-for-the-health-of-it.html#:~:text=In%20addition%2C%20medical%20research%20estimates,been%20linked%20to%20stress%20factors.

30 May Choy, "Emotion Regulation's Role in Relationship Quality: Comparisons Among American and Indian Committed Romantic Couples," repository.arizona.edu, May 2015, https://repository.arizona.edu/handle/10150/579398.

side benefit from being fully engaged empathetically is that we can exercise control over our emotions, taking care of our own stress and improving our health.

You have within you the power to believe that tomorrow can be better than today and that you can craft a plan to make it so. External events happen, and we can impact our own estimation of how over-whelmed we feel as a result.

If you are distressed by anything external, the pain is not due to the thing itself but to your own estimate of it; and this you have the power to revoke at any moment.

—MARCUS AURELIUS

Take Action:

- Think about a person you know who seems connected to others. What do you notice about their stress level?

- Observe the behaviors of famously centered people (e.g., Thich Nhat Hanh). What behaviors and practices do they engage in? Do you believe that empathy made them well or that being well caused them to be empathetic? Why or why not?

- **Radical Empathy:** It is often said that health = wealth. Studies reveal that wealth may be at odds with empathy and compassion. Research published in the journal Psychological Science found that people of modest economic means were better at reading others' facial expressions—an important marker of empathy—than wealthier people.[31] Has your income level changed? If so, how has that created a heart/compassion/empathy deficit? Increase?

---

31   Association for Psychological Science, "Rich less empathetic than poor, study says," psychologicalscience.org, September 30, 2011, https://www.psychologicalscience. org/news/rich-less-empathetic-than-poor-study-says.html.

DAY 2: PAY ATTENTION

Focus: Understanding people's emotions when you are with them. Paying attention to how other people are feeling can positively impact your relationships.

Effective communication skills are perhaps the most basic skills that you can possess and are essential to effective leadership, yet they remain one of the most sought after. Paying attention and trying to understand where other people are coming from can improve communication. Inattention and lack of empathy can cause people to misinterpret what other people are trying to say, which can lead to miscommunication, conflict, and damaged relationships.

People who express empathy are more likely to have healthy relationships. This is primarily because empathy can improve understanding when other people feel that their feelings and needs are important and being considered. It can also make it easier to form bonds and increase the likelihood that people receive meaningful help. When we decide to pay attention and attune to the needs of people around us, we must avoid judging and focus on helping. When people feel empathy for others, they behave in helpful ways. This can affect people on an individual level. Empathetic leaders can go beyond the individual and systemically impact groups, governments, and societies by leading with a deliberate demonstration of empathy toward people who need support.

Almost everything easy to mock turns out to be interesting if you pay closer attention.

—JOHN GREEN

Take Action:

- **Walking meditation:** Today notice the sensations of walking—your feet on the ground, the wind caressing your skin, sounds in the air, etc. Walking can take place either indoors or outdoors.

- **Focused body scan:** Starting with the head and ending at the toes, consider your body parts and the feelings you have. Tightness? Tingling? Warmth? Cold?

- **Radical Empathy:** Open monitoring: Learn to pay attention to what's happening around you without becoming attached to it. This practice is not about paying attention to a particular object or objects. Instead, it's about remaining open to any experience—internal or external—that arises and allowing it to wash over you. Don't process it; don't think about it. Just notice. To do this, sit comfortably in an upright position and try to be aware of any sensations, thoughts, or emotions that emerge without holding on to them. It may help you to label what comes up by using words like planning, future, judging, past. You can do this silently or out loud. After you name it, let it go. Do this for fifteen minutes. Pro tip: Resmaa Menakem has specific body exercises for racial healing in the body if you'd like to practice some of them.[32]

---

32 Resmaa Menakem, "Unlocking the Genius of Your Body," resmaa. com, December 18, 2020, https://www.resmaa.com/somatic-learnings/ unlocking-the-genius-of-your-body.

DAY 3: READ FICTION

Focus: Read fiction, allowing yourself to be transported into the book or article. Avoid violent movies, music, and video games, which are proven to reduce empathy and increase aggression.

Reading can't fix the world's problems, but it could help make it a more empathetic place. People who were assigned to read literary fiction showed the most improvement on empathy tests. People who read fiction tend to better understand and share in the feelings of others, even those who are different from them. Recent brain research suggests that reading literary fiction helps people develop empathy and critical thinking.[33] When we read, we strengthen our empathy muscles. Through fiction, we can experience the world as another gender, ethnicity, culture, sexuality, profession, or age. Words on a page can introduce us to what it's like to lose a child, be swept up in a war, be born into poverty, or leave home and emigrate to a new country. Taken together, this can influence how we relate to others in the real world.

As your imagination becomes more engaged and you connect emotionally to characters, you improve your ability to reflect on your own feelings, problems, and desires. Understanding your own feelings

---

33 Julianne Chiaet, "Novel Finding: Reading Literary Fiction Improves Empathy," sci-entificamerican.com, October 4, 2013, https://www.scientificamerican.com/article/novel-finding-reading-literary-fiction-improves-empathy/.

can help you feel more connected to other people and reduce depression or anxiety.

Fiction is the lie through which we tell the truth.

—ALBERT CAMUS

Take Action:

- Listen to an excerpt from the children's literary fiction book *Mama's Nightingale.*

- What memory from an experience (childhood or recent) came up for you as you listened to the story? Did you imagine yourself as the child or separate and apart from the child? What impact do you think that has on your ability to empathize with the character's experience?

- **Radical Empathy:** Consider your personal responsibility to teach empathy to other people. You can find many works of fiction that can help build your empathy. You can even find age-appropriate books for your children. Bonus points if you pick fiction books by authors who represent diverse communities.

DAY 4: FEEDBACK

Focus: Learn to accept positive and negative feedback with the same level of grace. Ask people to share the ways your thinking, your leadership, your parenting, or your service can be better.

Empathy is accepting that people have individual opinions. Your job is to listen and accept their opinion without judgment. **Acceptance is different from agreeing with that opinion.** Without judgment, gratitude for the feedback will come more naturally. When a person speaks up, especially providing critical or constructive feedback, they're taking a risk and being vulnerable. Don't get defensive.

Feedback is a process, and it may be difficult the first or second time you're in a feedback conversation to truly express gratitude and actively listen. It will get easier over time. You're growing, changing, and improving all the time as an individual and as a leader. To continue doing so, you'll need ongoing feedback. Receiving it well makes it more likely people will provide feedback in the future.

More importantly, restate the feedback you heard, allowing the other person to feel seen, heard, and supported in the conversation. It confirms for them that the conversation isn't a waste of their time. It is an empathetic act to understand and care about other people's experience. The more we have empathy, the more we are attuned to what's really going on for them. This allows for better communication and mutual understanding that can build the relationship.

Examine what is said and not who speaks.

—AFRICAN PROVERB

Take Action:

- Practice saying only "Thank you for sharing" when you receive criticism or feedback.

- Restate what you hear before responding to feedback or criticism to check your own understanding of the message.

- **Radical Empathy:** Notice when you tend to get defensive about feedback. What themes are present when you feel defensive? What are you telling yourself about the feedback giver? In what ways are you receptive to feedback based on who is giving the feedback? What are you feeling about yourself? What does this new knowledge reveal about where you tend to avoid being empathetic to yourself and others? What's one thing you can do to improve?

DAY 5: INTERCONNECTED MINDFULNESS

Focus: Concentrate on being intensely aware of what you're sensing and feeling in the moment without interpretation or judgment. Extend this awareness to communities where you belong.

Mindfulness involves breathing methods, guided imagery, and other practices to relax the body and mind and help reduce stress. However, mindfulness isn't simply about sharpening attention. When we practice mindfulness, we are simultaneously strengthening our skills of compassion.

Regular practice increases empathy and compassion for others and for oneself, and such attitudes are good for you. Compassion toward ourselves is intertwined with being more compassionate toward others. As we show kindness, openness, and curiosity toward ourselves, it builds the self-compassion that helps foster compassion toward others.

Dr. Shauna Shapiro says another way that mindfulness cultivates compassion is that it helps us recognize our interconnectedness.[34] For example, imagine that your hand has a splinter in it. Wouldn't you use your other hand to pull the splinter out? The left hand wouldn't say to the right hand, "Oh, thank you so much! You're so compassionate

---

34 Shauna Shapiro, "How Mindfulness Cultivates Compassion," Greater Good Science Center, January 28, 2014, YouTube, https://www.youtube.com/watch?v=_WGM1vGLLSQ.

and generous!" The right hand's removing the splinter is simply the appropriate response—it's just what the right hand does, because the two hands are part of the same body. Empathy is engaging in the most appropriate responses. The more you practice mindfulness, the more you begin to behave as if we are all part of the same body.

> The more you practice mindfulness, the more you begin to behave as if we are all part of the same body.

Communication leads to community, that is, to understanding, intimacy and mutual valuing.

—DR. ROLLO MAY

Take Action:

- What "bodies" or communities do you belong to?

- What other communities are impacted by the communities you are a part of?

- **Radical Empathy:** Create Truth Racial Healing & Transformation in Your Community. Too often people resolve that racial healing and progress cannot be obtained. As such they avoid earnest efforts to create a path forward.

DAY 6: READ THE ROOM

Focus: Notice when connection or disconnection is occurring.

To "read the table" means to scan all the people around a conference table quickly and discreetly when entering a meeting to gauge or assess the general demeanor of the attendees. Similarly, to "read the room" means to do the same thing but in a larger sense. "Read the room" is a colloquial expression for understanding the thoughts, relations, emotions, and stances of various people in the same place. Observing how an audience is responding can help you adjust in real time, address any objections, or invite questions. Being able to engage and respond to people appropriately and build trust and rapport can be particularly important when communicating and building empathy.[35]

Sometimes you can almost feel a shift in people's attention. They might start looking at their watches or cellphones, indicating they are ready to leave. Or something you say might provoke people to shut down or have an angry outburst. If you observe this occurring, you should respond to the changing situation rather than continue talking or shutting down yourself without acknowledging the shift. You might say something like, "I can tell you didn't like my last comments, so let's talk about it." Or if the other person needs more time to think,

---

35   Marcus Lemonis, "10 Reasons Why Business Communication Matters," marcus-lemonis.com, September 20, 2022, https://www.marcuslemonis.com/business/why-business-communication-matters.

you could say, "Let me know what you thought about my comments, and we can continue our conversation in a few days."

It's hard to notice things without people noticing me and that takes some getting used to.

—EDIE FALCO

Take Action:

- Be a social spy. You can discreetly observe, hold back, and take an inventory of the group or situation's mood, tone, members, energy, etc.

- Role-play entering different situations and decoding what's going on. Identify some things you will look for when reading the room.

- **Radical Empathy:** Take the Reading the Mind in the Eyes test at http://socialintelligence.labinthewild.org/mite/. What do you think about your results? How can you use this information to become an even more empathetic person? How do you think the results might change based on similarities or differences such as race, gender, etc.?

DAY 7: EXPOSURE

Focus: Practice empathy toward viewpoints that are not your own. Try following media or religious or cultural practices that vary from your own.

The theory of mind, which is a concept related to empathy, refers to our ability to comprehend that other people hold beliefs and desires and that they might be different from our own. Cultures that tend to be more collectivistic tend to have higher levels of empathy. Collectivism involves seeing oneself as being part of a larger, interconnected group of familial and other close relationships, with a priority on fitting in with others and maintaining harmony. The United States has the lowest collectivism score of any nation, but don't fret. US citizens can develop empathy despite being individualistic.

It is important to think about how indifference and a lack of exposure can be limiting in your own lives. If you aren't empathetic and open to working and having relationships with people with different lived experiences, you limit the options you have in life. Like-minded people are less likely to stretch you beyond your current thinking.

All humans share common traits. While it's important to understand cultural diversity, acknowledging common traits across cultures can also help you develop empathy. Uncovering what we have in common with someone from a different culture can make others seem more familiar, which will increase feelings of comfort across cultural differences.

If the ideas are not exposed to other people in the world, those ideas don't do us any good.

—POOJA AGNIHOTRI

Take Action:

- For five minutes, watch or listen to news outside your norm for the sole purpose of being exposed rather than to debate the merits of what you hear.

- What happened to your body? In your mind?

- **Radical Empathy:** Schedule to have coffee or a drink with a family member or neighbor or someone else you have been in a relationship with in the past but whom you stopped talking to because of a difference of opinion. Note: You can choose not to reconcile, but check to be certain that you have worked through the issue.

Week Two:

Practice Empathy

DAY 1: VULNERABILITY

Focus: Embrace uncertainty. Take risks. Risk emotional exposure.

Emotional vulnerability is the ability or willingness to acknowledge and/or express emotions, particularly those emotions that are challenging, like shame, sadness, anxiety, or insecurity. Vulnerability is closely tied to empathy. Without vulnerability, we can't access our own experiences that allow us to be empathetic. We also can't share important personal moments so that others can relate to us.

Dr. Brené Brown shares that empathy is not possible without vulnerability; only sympathy is. Sympathy, or feeling sorry for someone, can drive disconnection. Sympathy is not bad. It may even cause me to feel closer to you. However, empathy fuels connection: I am you. Dr. Brown says that empathy is a vulnerable choice because in order to connect with you, I must connect with something in myself that knows that feeling. Empathy is about being present with someone, and if you are present and engaged and take the armor off, you'll know what a person needs.

Human connection makes things better for people. When vulnerability is added to empathy, the result is connection or community. You cannot *do* empathy alone. We get our empathy from other people. They expand my empathy by giving me theirs, and I acknowledge their humanity by being empathetic. Babies are brought into the human community by bringing forth their parents' empathy and becoming socialized by it. Students spark their teachers' empathy and are educated through it—brought into the educated community. The list goes on.

Embrace your vulnerability and celebrate your flaws; it will let you appreciate the world around you and make you more compassionate.

—MASABA GUPTA

Take Action:

- Share with someone something personal about yourself that you would normally hold back.

- Tell someone when they do something to upset you.

- **Radical Empathy:** Think about something that you are ashamed of and that people know about. Perhaps it is something that is a matter of public record, such as a lawsuit, a divorce, or a termination. Maybe it's something else. Practice being the one to bring it up.

DAY 2: STOP NUMBING

Focus: Allow yourself to feel negative emotions, like grief, disappointment, fear, pain, and hurt. You cannot selectively numb emotion. When you numb those feelings, you also numb the feel-good emotions, like gratitude, happiness, and joy.

The human mind is not particularly good at thinking about and empathizing with millions or billions of individuals. As the number of victims in a tragedy increases, our empathy and our willingness to help reliably decreases. We care a lot about individuals. We feel a strong emotional response when we see a person in danger or a single abandoned animal. But research shows that as problems grow and more people suffer, our emotional response doesn't scale up. This is especially true when the numbers are shared in the form of statistics. It is called "psychic numbing," and it tells us a lot about the way we respond, or don't respond, to some of the world's biggest problems.

This is an adaptive response. When overwhelmed with loss, trauma, and sorrow, people will grow numb to feelings. But awareness is the first step in any change. I wish I knew an easier path to change, one that didn't start with the excruciating process of waking up. If we are numb, it is because the alternative is horror or terror. So we must begin by noticing when we are numb and knowing that terror lies sleeping underneath. The good news is that terror or fear does not mean that we are unsafe. We mustn't allow fear to cause us to become calloused.

There are people behind each data point. Focus on the people behind the numbers.

Even partial solutions can save whole lives.

—PAUL SLOVIC

Take Action:

- Celebrate when large groups of people experience joy.

- When have you turned away when you learned of large groups of people experiencing pain or suffering? In what ways can you acknowledge the hurt?

- **Radical Empathy:** Contribute to an effort that feels gargantuan and you don't know how to fix it.

DAY 3: DITCH PERFECTION

Focus: You are imperfect, and that is enough. This "I would never!" position is not helpful.

Here's an exercise designed to cultivate empathy.

Close your eyes and imagine someone drastically different from you. Perhaps they are standing on the side of the road, dirty, ragged, and tired, begging for money. Or maybe it is somebody you recently read about who committed an unthinkable crime. Take your time and visualize them in as much detail as you can.

Notice how your body responds to the imagery.

Now, ask yourself, What would have happened to cause me to be in that position? If you're like most, your first thought will likely be an indignant

I would never!

I can't even!

That's okay. Now, answer the question, What could have happened to this individual that would lead them to such profound despair? Go back in time and imagine yourself as this person. What was living like one, five, ten years ago? Ask yourself what your parents were like. Did they have the ability to show morality or fairness? Did they show you tenderness? Did they care about you?

Have you imagined that being assaulted, beaten, or humiliated has brought you to this point? How did it change you? Have you been hungry, and how did it change you? Now, visualize the person the day they were born. Are they different from your child or the child of a friend? Probably not. They had the same vulnerability, the same innate needs, and the same intrinsic curiosity and joy that we all do.

Check in with your body again and notice if/how your sensory experience has changed.

Perfection is the enemy of authenticity.
—LISA BRAITHWAITE

Take Action:

- In what ways do you need to stop holding yourself to a standard of perfection?

- How can you extend that same grace to other people?

- **Radical Empathy:** Reduce your social media use. Social media contributes to frequent social comparison, which can worsen perfectionism. Try taking a break from technology for a half or full day and see how you feel. When you start using social media after the break, notice how you feel. Are you engaging in social comparison and feeling "not good enough" or feeling like other people aren't good enough either? If so, consider implementing a regular break from social media a few times per week.

DAY 4: REMEMBER GRACE

Focus: Stop practicing revisionist history. There has been a point in your life where someone granted you grace even if they were unable to empathize with you.

Sometimes it's hard to have empathy. Empathy requires experience, and until we've walked in another person's shoes, we may find it difficult or impossible to understand the emotions they are experiencing or why they do the things they do. It isn't fair to judge others based on our own experiences, but we do it all the time. This is not because we are bad people but because we lack empathy. We can filter things only through the context of our own reality. So how are we to offer others genuine and sincere understanding all the time?

The answer is this: We can't. And that's okay.

We often find it easier to show empathy with children. When children are sad or afraid, we offer them grace and reassurance. Empathy comes easily because we all remember when we were sad or scared as kids. But as adults, when other adults are sad or fearful, too often we belittle, ridicule, or tease.

In adulthood we are expected to always move forward fearlessly and with confidence. But things outside our realm of experience or comfort zone can still be fear inducing or scary. If we cannot relate to another adult's grief or fear or don't understand how they feel, we should offer them grace and kindness instead of calling them irrational or silly or saying they are overreacting.

What may seem irrational to you is perfectly rational to someone else. They aren't necessarily irrational. It's simply how they experience the world. Don't punish others for not experiencing the world in the same way you do. Empathy requires experience sometimes. Grace needs only practice.

This practice is easier if you try to recall when someone else has offered you grace.

> *Grace is a power that comes in and transforms*
> *a moment into something better.*
>
> —CAROLINE MYSS

Take Action:

- Think of a time when someone gave you an opportunity or a second chance when you did not deserve it. Document the event. What details had you forgotten?

- Describe this event to another person.

- **Radical Empathy:** Look for opportunities to give other people multiple chances to grow and develop. If you struggle doing so with adults, start practicing with younger people.

DAY 5: FORGIVE

Focus: Holding a grudge can weigh you down, and it's just not worth the suffering. Developing empathy is a necessary step in forgiveness.

The positive emotions that lead to forgiveness have been identified as empathy, sympathy, compassion, and love. Having greater empathy makes it easier to forgive than having little to no empathy. For many people, finding empathy for those who have hurt us is difficult. Understandably so. No one wants to take the point of view of someone they resent or fear. Why would anyone want to envision the life of the wrongdoer whose values are fundamentally different from our own? Sometimes people do not respond with empathy toward a person who is suffering, especially when they feel the person deserves punishment.

When people do something that hurts you, they often react in several ways: guilt, indifference, minimization, or shame. If the wrongdoer can empathize, they will be able to imagine and feel the events that unfolded from your point of view. Even if they don't evaluate what happened the same, they are more likely to feel bad for the impact and take corrective action. These conciliatory behaviors obliterate guilt, making self-forgiveness more likely.

> Self-forgiveness is an empathetic act, regardless of whether you are the wrongdoer or the person wronged.

Someone who cannot think about circumstances from other vantage points has a much harder time recognizing

184

either the need for self-forgiveness or a path forward through self-healing. Self-forgiveness is an empathetic act, regardless of whether you are the wrongdoer or the person wronged.

When have you done something that required forgiveness?

Close your eyes and imagine the hurt of the person you wronged.

If you're sincere and take your time, you will have embodied our common humanity—empathy—if only fleetingly. You will discover that we are all responding to life with the inner and outer resources available to us. We are doing the best we can to navigate our path through a sometimes seemingly senseless existence. What a gift you own to have the awareness to choose healing and wholeness over suffering.

"You're not important enough to have a stranglehold on me." It's saying, "You don't get to trap me in the past. I am worthy of a future."

—JODI PICOULT

Take Action:

- Try to understand the motives behind people's actions.

- What's one thing that people have misunderstood about you? In what way would they better understand if you were able to explain your motivations?

- **Radical Empathy:** Choose battles wisely. Not every transgression deserves a reaction. In other words, not every bad or hurtful action requires forgiveness. Some things are just too insignificant to worry about. For our own peace of mind, some things are better left alone. By exercising empathy and managing our expectations, we can do this more efficiently. Think about what you need to simply let go. Then let it go.

DAY 6: BE BRAVE

Focus: Courage is the choice and willingness to confront agony, pain, danger, uncertainty, or intimidation. Being willing to risk the discomfort is true vulnerability. We can measure how courageous you are based on how vulnerable you are.

People wonder how empathy and bravery are connected. Let's consider this question in light of a scenario.

Imagine a workplace bully verbally attacking another coworker. As an observer, there are three emotions that you may experience.

1. **Indifference or Fear:** If you do not have empathy, you may find yourself on the spectrum of apathy, choosing to remain distant and ignore the situation at hand. You may be afraid of the consequences of some harm befalling you. Fear is our brain's way of keeping us (and our species) alive. This emotion is regulated in a part of our brain called the amygdala. It handles innate reactions that we have about the world around us, especially things that might harm us. An overactive amygdala can shut down or limit access to empathy.

2. **Revenge or Mirroring:** On the other end of the spectrum, you might care only about yourself and have a selfish desire to mirror the bully's behavior. You might want to put the bully down so you can take some form of revenge. This could be seen as an act of bullying too.

3. **Empathy:** When you are empathetic, you will feel the pain and suffering of the person but without any accompanying selfish interests. This is the empathy that every brave person must have. It takes courage to step out of your own shoes and to put yourself in another's shoes and to feel the hurt they are experiencing.

Why is it difficult for us to empathize with other people? What makes it so difficult for us to understand or share another person's experiences, feelings, or beliefs? Can you listen to someone who supports candidate so-and-so? Someone addicted to heroin? A military veteran? Women who have had multiple abortions? People who support the death penalty? Those who chant "Black lives matter"? "Blue lives matter"? What are the feelings you have about the associations or lack of similarities between the types of people mentioned?

Can you sit down, with mutual respect, and discuss drastically different outlooks on life? It is possible to understand another person's perspective without compromising your own feelings and thoughts about life. It is possible to consider someone else's perspective without having to agree or disagree with it. It is possible to listen with imagination. The bottom line is, there is courage gained in understanding others. This contradicts the myth that one's ability to care for and then understand others is a sign of being submissive. On the contrary, you must be a brave person to do so.

> *I think we all have empathy [but] we may*
> *not have enough courage to display it.*
>
> —MAYA ANGELOU

Take Action:

- What friendship do you have that would surprise people? What impact has this friendship had on you and your beliefs?

- If asked, do you think the person you describe would list you among their cadre of friendships?

- **Radical Empathy:** Think about a hobby you have and make a conscious effort to invite someone unlike you to join you, or, better yet, join them while they engage in one of theirs.

DAY 7: GO FIRST

Focus: Expecting someone else to show empathy before you will is not empathetic.

Quid pro quo means that you have an expectation of goods or services in exchange for your money, goods, or services. It is not an empathetic gesture. When you give of yourself and expect something in return, it's a transaction. You have one eye on your actions and the other on what you'll get in return. Not only does that take you away from the moment, but you can't do your best or be your best when you have a hidden agenda.

Picking and choosing who to be empathetic toward is not empathy. Empathy is a more global element of a person's character that allows one in all situations to see things from another's point of view. Selective empathy is an oxymoron.

When we view our relationships and interactions as investments, we will seek returns as often as possible. When you give a gift, you automatically tell your mind and heart that you are full and don't hold any ill will or bad feelings toward that person. It's just like forgiveness—people don't always deserve it, but we forgive because it gives us freedom and helps us let go of anger and bitterness.

Be the change you want to see.

—MAHATMA GANDHI

190

Take Action:

- Document three things that you want to continue now that the fourteen-day assignment is over.

- Choose one thing that you will do on a regular basis to build your empathy muscle.

- **Radical Empathy:** Share with people in your networks the one thing you are committing to with the hashtag #empathyrevolution

I Got Work to Do

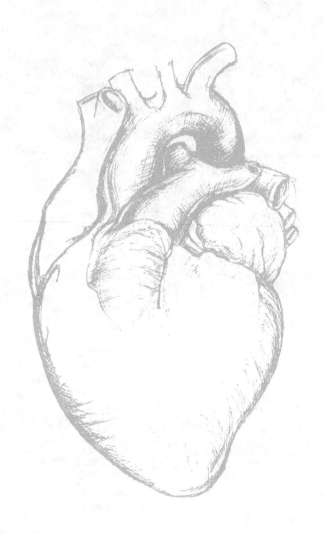

I will be the first one to tell you that shifting from objectivity to greater levels of empathy is not easy. Now that I am on the other side of my journey, I do feel like it is not that complicated. Every day, people I know and many I don't know look to me for empathy and compassion. They tell me stories of their grandchildren being ill. They share fears about relationships ending. People share with me their greatest desires as they age. Today, I can look at a person and feel when they are not okay. It was quite draining when it first started to happen. Then someone introduced me to a book about healing racial trauma in the body: *My Grandmother's Hands: Racialized Trauma and the Pathway to Mending Our Hearts and Bodies*. If you are not a reader, it is not a book you really need to read. What's more important is that you complete the dozens of trauma-healing exercises in the book. If you don't care about racial trauma or healing, no need to worry about that either. The exercises still work. I have found that these somatic body exercises help me to handle the issues of other people without feeling like I am going to crash with them.

I am a person of great faith, and so I practice the tenets of my faith tradition as well. It feels irresponsible to ask you to take this empathetic journey without warning you that you will need some coping strategies. If you happen to be agnostic or an atheist, that's not a problem. Just know that you need an outlet for the receiving energy you will give off. I swear to you that I feel like I have a sign painted on my forehead that says "Tell me how I can help you today." Occasionally, it gets to be overwhelming. I still have lots of work to do. However, I sleep well, exercise, and try to eat real food and get some sunshine and all the other things that doctors tell us can lead to a healthy lifestyle. These things have been my saving grace. I cannot emphasize enough that you will need some strategies, too, if you want to do more than just cope. The goal is to thrive as your improved empathetic self. Because I've got so much work to do, I invite you to share your stories and best practices with me at www.drnicoleprice. com.

One last thing: I am still probably the worst person to author a book about empathy, but here we are.

About the Author

Dr. Nicole Price is a leadership consultant and professional speaker. Each year she speaks to thousands of people on related leadership topics, like empathy, inclusion and belonging, change management, and style. She is currently the human rights commissioner for the City of Kansas City, Missouri, in the United States of America.

Each year in August, she welcomes more people to join the empathy revolution. If you are interested, please visit www.drnicole-price.com. There you will find resources for businesses, nonprofits, school districts, faith-based organizations, and individuals to help build more empathy muscle in the world. There you will also find information for how to register for the Empathy Revolution Institute.

Nicole is also the CEO of Lively Paradox, a Midwest-based consulting firm that specializes in "helping difference get along." Lively Paradox offers professional services that include the following:

- Leadership development training and consulting
- Team retreat sessions
- Diversity, equity, and inclusion services

If you would like to connect with Dr. Price directly, call 800-914-9205, and someone will ensure you can chat with her.

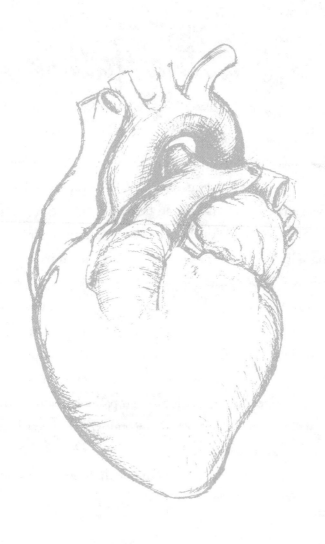